Sustainable Development:
A Canadian Perspective

NIAGARA COLLEGE LRC

**National Library of Canada cataloguing
in publication data**

Main entry under title:
Sustainable Development: A Canadian Perspective

Issued also in French under title:
Le Canada et le développement durable

ISBN 0-662-32582-6
Cat. no. En40-668/2002E

1. Sustainable development–Canada.
2. Environmental protection–Canada.
3. Environmental policy–Canada.
4. Canada. Environment Canada.

HC120.S87 2002   333.7'2'0971   C2002-980192-3

Reprinted April 2003

PREFACE

Through August 26 – September 4, 2002, participants will gather in Johannesburg, South Africa, for the World Summit on Sustainable Development.

The Summit provides an opportunity to reinvigorate the global commitment towards the achievement of sustainable development.

Sustainable Development: A Canadian Perspective was commissioned by the Government of Canada through the Earth Summit 2002 Canadian Secretariat, as part of Canada's preparations for the Summit. It is neither a checklist nor a report card. Rather, it involved collecting views on accomplishments and challenges from different segments of society to provide a perspective on Canada's progress towards sustainable development over the past decade. The paper highlights some of Canada's considerable successes, speaks of some of the remaining challenges and explores some of the current efforts underway to meet those challenges.

The report is the result of a broad based process that included contributions from experts both inside and outside government, as well as public input through a series of cross-Canada roundtable discussions. A draft of the report was posted on the Earth Summit 2002 Canadian Secretariat website.

The Government of Canada gratefully acknowledges the contributions of all these participants.

TABLE OF CONTENTS

1 INTRODUCTION 1
    1.1 Overview 1
    1.2 Economy 1
    1.3 Governance 2
    1.4 Social and Cultural Diversity 3
    1.5 Canada in the Global Context 6

2 CHANGES TO DECISION-MAKING STRUCTURES AND PROCESSES 8
    2.1 Governments 8
    2.2 Corporate Initiatives 14
    2.3 Non-Governmental Organizations 17
    2.4 Labour 18
    2.5 Education for Sustainable Development 19
    2.6 Continuing Challenges 21

3 SOCIAL SUSTAINABILITY 22
    3.1 Social Investment 22
    3.2 Budgetary Measures 23
    3.3 Eradicating Poverty 24
    3.4 Regional Equity 26
    3.5 Gender Equity 26
    3.6 Aboriginal People 27
    3.7 Continuing Challenges 32

4 SUSTAINABLE COMMUNITIES 33
    4.1 Urban Communities 33
    4.2 Rural Canada 37
    4.3 International Initiatives 38
    4.4 Continuing Challenges 39

5 HEALTH AND ENVIRONMENT 40
    5.1 Air 41
    5.2 Water 44
    5.3 Toxic Substances 48
    5.4 Continuing Challenges 51

Sustainable Development: A Canadian Perspective

6 CONSERVATION AND STEWARDSHIP OF BIODIVERSITY 52

    6.1   Background 52

    6.2   Identification, Monitoring, and Systematization 52

    6.3   Endangered Species 54

    6.4   Protected Areas 57

    6.5   Stewardship 61

    6.6   Continuing Challenges 62

7 SUSTAINABLE DEVELOPMENT OF NATURAL RESOURCES 64

    7.1   Forests 64

    7.2   Mining 72

8 CLIMATE CHANGE 80

    8.1   Mitigation 81

    8.2   Research and Studies 85

    8.3   Adaptation 86

    8.4   Continuing Challenges 90

9 THE CANADIAN ARCTIC 91

    9.1   Background 91

    9.2   Political Development 94

    9.3   Economic Development 95

    9.4   Continuing Challenges 97

10 INTERNATIONAL COOPERATION 99

    10.1   Trade and Sustainable Development 100

    10.2   Canadian Development Cooperation – Financing 102

    10.3   Canadian Development Cooperation – Focus 104

    10.4   Basic Human Needs and Social Development 105

    10.5   Environment 106

    10.6   Desertification 107

    10.7   Continuing Challenges 107

11 CONCLUSION 108

1 INTRODUCTION

1.1 OVERVIEW

Canada is the world's second-largest country. Covering half a continent, bordering on three oceans and intersected by six time zones, this vast country is characterized by its geographical, climatic, economic and social diversity. Canada's landscape includes fertile plains in the western provinces, rugged mountain ranges in the West, a vast boreal forest, the Arctic tundra in the far North, the Canadian shield of rock and lakes in eastern and central Canada, and some of the Earth's largest lakes and longest rivers.

There are many climatic variations in this huge country, ranging from the permanently frozen icecaps north of the 70th parallel to the luxuriant vegetation of British Columbia's west coast. Canada's most populous regions lie in the country's south along the U.S. border and enjoy four distinct seasons. Here, daytime summer temperatures can rise to 35°C and higher, while lows of minus 25°C are not uncommon in winter.

Canada's population is approximately 30.7 million. A large majority of this population is urban, with a third of it concentrated in four major cities: Toronto, Montreal, Vancouver and Ottawa (the national capital).

Because of the great diversity in climates, landform, vegetation, resources and economic activities, environmental stresses vary considerably across the country. In the boreal zones, some of the main concerns include ensuring sustainable use of forests and non-polluting mining operations. In agricultural and urban-based regions such as the Prairies, the Great Lakes and St. Lawrence Valley, and parts of the west coast, concerns include polluted drinking water, urban congestion, air pollution, and loss of both wildlife habitat and farmland. On both coasts, declining fish stocks and concerns regarding forestry practices and land-based pollution are also significant. In the Arctic, prime concerns are managing the impacts of resource development on a fragile ecosystem, and reducing the contamination of wildlife and 'country' food sources by toxic substances emitted from distant sources. The effects of climate change are also increasingly being felt in Canada's North.

1.2 ECONOMY

Canada ranks sixth in the world in gross domestic product per capita. While much of Canada's wealth and material well-being is based on its rich endowment of natural resources such as forests, fossil fuels and other minerals, there are significant regional differences in Canada's economy: resource extractive industries are relatively more important in the east, west and north; agriculture plays an important role in the three prairie provinces; and manufacturing and services fuel Ontario's and Quebec's economy.

Trade is the lifeblood of the Canadian economy, with exports accounting for more than 40 per cent of the Gross Domestic Product (GDP), making Canada one of the most open economies in the world. Canada's leading exports are automobile vehicles and parts, machinery and equipment, high-technology products, oil, natural gas, metals, and forest and farm products. Canada and the United States have the largest and most comprehensive trading relationship in the world. Two-way trade between these two countries is now US$1.3 billion a day. More than 80 per cent of all Canadian exports go to the U.S, while nearly a quarter of US exports come to Canada. Canada's exports to the U.S. and Mexico rose by 110 per cent between 1993 and 2000, driven by the North American Free Trade Agreement (NAFTA).

Canadian governments collectively undertook major economic reforms during the course of the 1990s, generating significant public debate on the appropriate role of government. Aside from NAFTA, the most noteworthy initiative was the elimination of large budgetary deficits at both the federal and provincial levels. In addition, federal and some provincial governments restructured services, reduced transfer payments and subsidies and cut regulations in some cases. As well, taxes have been lowered in a number of jurisdictions. Following these efforts, some governments have begun to reinvest in priority areas, including health and addressing child poverty.

1.3 GOVERNANCE

Canada is a constitutional monarchy and a federal state (with ten provinces, three territories and a number of self-governing Aboriginal communities) with a democratic system of government. The Canadian constitution divides powers between the federal and provincial governments, giving the federal government jurisdiction over such matters as interprovincial and international trade, foreign affairs, communications, criminal law, fisheries, and Aboriginal affairs. Provincial government jurisdiction is over matters such as property and civil rights, local works and undertakings, municipal institutions and the development and management of natural resources. The federal and provincial governments exercise concurrent powers over agriculture.

Although constitutional dependents of the federal government, the three territories are gradually acquiring powers similar to those of the provinces. Constitutionally protected land claim and self-government agreements completed with some First Nations and Inuit recognize the inherent right of Aboriginal peoples to govern their own affairs, including the area of environment. Not explicitly mentioned in the Constitution, the environment has emerged as an area of shared jurisdiction. While social policy falls under provincial jurisdiction, the federal government has played an important role in funding various social programs since the Second World War.

The shared nature of environmental jurisdiction makes close cooperation among the federal, provincial, territorial and Aboriginal governments vital to the success of national environmental policies and objectives. To develop national policies and standards to address issues of common concern such as climate change and biodiversity, a number of coordinating councils have been created in a variety of policy fields such as environment, energy, forestry, and protected areas. While this partnership is effective in most areas, differing views are created by environmental management and overlapping jurisdiction in policy-making and planning.

The division of responsibilities over environmental, social and economic policies among the federal, provincial, territorial and Aboriginal governments adds complexity to the pursuit of broad societal objectives and requires close coordination within and among governments, as well as with the private sector and civil society.

1.4 Social and Cultural Diversity

Canada has two official languages: English, the first language of 59 per cent of Canadians; and French, the first language of 23 per cent of the population. A full 18 per cent have either more than one mother tongue or a first language other than English or French. In Quebec, however, 81 per cent of the population is francophone, nine per cent is Anglophone and 10 per cent speak a first language other than French or English.

Canada is home to approximately 1.3 million Aboriginal people. There are over 50 distinct Aboriginal nations, speaking over 50 languages across the country, living in rural communities and urban centres. The existing Aboriginal and treaty rights of the Aboriginal people of Canada were entrenched in the Canadian *Constitution Act, 1982*. Aboriginal people are defined under Section 35 of the Constitution as including Indian (more commonly referred to now as First Nations, about 69 per cent of Canada's Aboriginal population), Inuit (five per cent), and Métis people (26 per cent).

Relations between the government and Aboriginal people are complex. The federal government has primary responsibility for Aboriginal affairs, but owing to provincial jurisdiction over land and resources, provincial/territorial activities often impact on Aboriginal people. As constitutional protection for Aboriginal and Treaty rights is a relatively recent phenomenon, both the government and Aboriginal peoples continue to debate the further definition of their respective rights and responsibilities.

Aboriginal peoples have lived close to the land for millennia. Aboriginal philosophies, cultures, spiritual practices, and customs are derived from this connection to the land. Some Aboriginal cultures have long held that any decision must be considered in light of its potential impact seven generations hence, a sentiment captured in the Brundtland definition of sustainable development. Many Aboriginal people, even in an urban setting, continue to pursue their traditions, though some are being lost, particularly languages. Owing to their close connection to the land, Aboriginal peoples are often the first to recognize changes to the environment and feel the impact of these changes.

Immigration is a significant factor in Canadian population growth and distribution. On a per capita basis, Canada is one of the countries that receives the most immigrants in the world. These immigrants have transformed Canadian society and made it a multi-cultural mosaic. Between 1992 and 2000, Canada received almost two million immigrants from all regions of the world.

Canada's economic, political and social diversity has led to many different points of view about how to promote sustainable development. While some have emphasized the importance of economic growth, others have underlined the need for comprehensive environmental protection, and still others have highlighted the need for increased equity in social conditions. Governments at all levels have put in place many processes to reconcile these different perspectives, but competing priorities have sometimes led to conflicting policies (such as urban development policies that lead to greater sprawl). How to reconcile economic and social imperatives with environmental needs remains a challenge in many policy areas.

CANADA'S RANKINGS IN INTERNATIONAL ENVIRONMENTAL COMPARISONS

Report Name & Year	Author of the report	Canada's overall rank	Canada's rank within the OECD	Canada's rank within the G-7
The Wellbeing of Nations: Ecosystem Wellbeing Index-2001	Robert Prescott-Allen in cooperation with several organizations[1]	94 / 180	3 / 30	1 / 7
Keeping Score- 2001	Friends of the Earth / *The Ecologist* journal	42 / 122	2 / 30	1 / 7
Canada versus the OECD- 2001	Eco-Research Chair, University of Victoria	28 / 29	28 / 29	6 / 7
Ecological Footprint (per capita score)	Redefining Progress / WWF International	141 / 151	23 / 30	6 / 7
Ecological Footprint (overall surplus / deficit score)	Redefining Progress / WWF International	13 / 151	2 / 30	1 / 7
Environmental Sustainability Index- 2002	World Economic Forum	4 / 122	4 / 30	1 / 7
Environmental Performance Index- 2002 (pilot)	World Economic Forum	6 / 23	6 / 23	1 / 7
Human Development Index	UNDP	3 / 162	3 / 30	1 / 7

International comparisons are inherently difficult because of data availability and comparison problems. The above studies vary significantly in what is measured and how the various measured issues are weighted. As a consequence, it is not surprising that overall results vary significantly. Taken together, the diverse results do not give a conclusive message. Canada generally ranks quite well overall compared to its peer countries, but does not rank as well when per capita measures are used.

---

[1] IUCN- The World Conservation Union, International Institute for Environment and Development, United Nations Food and Agriculture Organization, UNEP World Conservation Monitoring Centre.

Introduction

1.5 CANADA IN THE GLOBAL CONTEXT

At the dawn of the 21st Century, Canadians increasingly recognize that the country is intricately linked to others around the globe economically, environmentally and socially. As one of the most trade-dependent economies in the industrialized world, prosperity is increasingly linked to the global economy. Canada's vast geography makes it an importer of environmental problems (e.g, acid rain, stratospheric ozone depletion, persistent organic pollutants, climate change), just as a high consumption lifestyle makes it a contributor to such problems as wildlife habitat destruction, toxic wastes, greenhouse gas emissions, water and air pollution. As the events of September 2001 have demonstrated, Canada's security is linked to conflicts in regions of the globe that were once thought to be far away. For all these reasons, Canada has a stake in the sustainable development of the rest of the world along with responsibility as a wealthy and large per-capita resource user to introduce more sustainable forms of development domestically.

At the 1992 Earth Summit in Rio, Canada undertook, along with most other countries in the world, to work towards sustainable development. In the intervening decade, Canada's progress has been significant, but more needs to be done. While governments at all levels have made policy and institutional changes in order to promote more sustainable forms of development, while a large number of firms in the private sector have improved their environmental performance, while Canadians of all walks of life are more environmentally conscious, Canada as a whole is still at an early stage in its sustainable development journey.

There have been notable successes over the decade: Canadians enjoy a higher standard of living, a higher life expectancy, and are better educated than ever before; and governments have successfully controlled their deficits, tamed inflation and presided over a long period of economic expansion. On the environmental front, there has been a significant increase in protected areas, large-scale recycling programs have cut municipal solid wastes, the amount of toxic substances being released to the environment has declined, and the efficiency with which energy is used has improved (with the notable exception of the transportation sector). However, there have also been setbacks: Canadian emissions of greenhouse gases (GHG) have continued to increase; important fisheries have had to be closed; urban smog is getting worse; Canadian economic productivity continues to lag behind its major competitor; poverty levels have remained stubbornly even; and there remain great challenges to ensure improved quality of life for Aboriginal people.

Canada has experienced some painful lessons concerning the economic and social impacts of ignoring ecological constraints or failing to provide effective mechanisms to address competing social priorities concerning natural resources. The collapse of the Atlantic cod fishery and heated disputes over logging of old-growth forests have prompted some important policy changes. Nevertheless, the wrestle continues with fundamental issues related to the intersection of environmental, economic and social considerations.

This report provides an overview of Canada's major environmental, social and economic developments over the last decade. In order to keep it to a manageable length, the report is deliberately selective, with some issues receiving more coverage than others. Although they make a real contribution to Canada's sustainable development, many worthwhile initiatives, at the local level in particular, are not mentioned. The majority of this report focuses on domestic developments, but it also includes Canadian efforts in international cooperation: in an increasingly interdependent world, Canada cannot achieve its economic, environmental, health, peace and security objectives unless the rest of the world is also more prosperous, secure, equitable and environmentally sustainable.

2 CHANGES TO DECISION-MAKING STRUCTURES AND PROCESSES

2.1 GOVERNMENTS

At its core, sustainable development is about changing the way decisions are made, and ultimately the decisions themselves. Over the past decade, Canadian governments at all levels (federal, provincial, territorial, municipal and Aboriginal) have made important structural, procedural and policy changes in an effort to integrate environmental, social and economic values better into policies and programs and to reflect the views of stakeholders more effectively. As each of these governments has reflected its own circumstances and priorities, no single Canadian model has emerged. It is fair to say that, while governments have acted on many fronts, they are still learning and experimenting. As a result, no single focus has emerged at the national level for the range of efforts being undertaken at the federal, provincial and territorial levels. The examples below, therefore, are meant to illustrate the range of reforms undertaken and do not provide a comprehensive overview of what each jurisdiction is doing.

a) Promoting greater policy coherence

Developing policies that reinforce economic, environmental and social objectives remains a challenge although several governments have made changes in both organizational structure (by merging resource ministries into sustainable development ministries, giving expanded mandates to existing ministries or creating new permanent advisory bodies on sustainable development) and in policy processes (by introducing more comprehensive environmental assessment requirements or by broadening public consultation processes). At the federal level, the *1999 Cabinet Directive on the Environmental Assessment of Policy, Plan and Program Proposals* requiring departments to prepare an environmental assessment of a policy, plan or program proposal that is submitted to a Minister or Cabinet for approval, and the preparation of departmental sustainable development strategies (see below) are examples of processes designed to promote greater policy coherence.

> ### Strategic Land Use Planning In British Columbia
>
> Strategic land use planning in British Columbia involves all levels of government, First Nations and a wide range of stakeholders, including the forest industry, environmental groups and tourism interests. To date, three regional and 15 sub-regional plans covering 73 per cent of the province have been completed. The outcomes of approved strategic land use plans are:
>
> - the resolution of land use issues;
> - a range of resource management zones that support investment certainty by defining where resource development can occur and to what extent;
> - protected areas that protect the natural diversity of the province and recreational features;
> - agricultural land zoning;
> - settlement zones for the future needs of local communities; and
> - information contributing to forest certification.

b) *Leadership by example*

The federal government and several provinces have committed themselves to environmental excellence in their own operations. Among other things, they have introduced recycling programs and environmental guidelines in procurement, increased the energy efficiency of their buildings and vehicle fleets, and have begun to purchase "green" electricity from renewable sources. While the direct impact of such measures is limited, they are important both symbolically and for their demonstration value.

c) *Changes in accountability practices*

The federal government has established a Commissioner of the Environment and Sustainable Development within the Office of the Auditor General. Among other activities, the Commissioner's Office reports annually to Parliament on the Government's progress in meeting its environment and sustainable development responsibilities, and oversees a petition process enabling the public to seek explanation from a Minister as to his or her decision on an environment or sustainable development issue. Under its Environmental Bill of Rights, Ontario has also created an independent Environmental Commissioner.

Under the Environmental Bill of Rights, citizens of Ontario have the right to comment on government proposals, appeal certain government decisions, ask for a review of current laws or request an investigation if they think someone is breaking a significant environmental law.

The Environmental Commissioner of Ontario reports annually to the provincial legislature on the implementation of the Environmental Bill of Rights, including Ministerial compliance with its provisions, and key issues of concern. Environmental assessment laws have been enacted by the federal and provincial governments, such as the *Canadian Environmental Assessment Act* that came into force in 1995, requiring the assessment of environmental effects before irrevocable decisions are made.

The Citizen Submissions on Enforcement Matters mechanism enables the public to "blow the whistle" when a government appears to be failing to enforce its environmental laws effectively. This was established under Article 14 of the North American Agreement on Environmental Cooperation (the first environmental agreement to an international trade agreement, signed as part of NAFTA–the North American Free Trade Agreement). Since its creation, the Secretariat has received ten submissions from Canadians alleging failure on enforcement of some of Canada's environmental laws. While the Secretariat has no power to compel a remedy, the creation of a public factual record can encourage the government concerned to enforce its environmental laws more effectively.

In addition, a growing number of federal, provincial and territorial environmental statutes incorporate "whistle-blower" provisions and authorize citizen suits to redress environmental violations.

d) *Incorporation of sustainable development into policy development and programs*

When the federal government amended the *Auditor General Act* in 1995 to create the office of the Commissioner of the Environment and Sustainable Development, it also required most federal departments to prepare Sustainable Development Strategies every three years and report annually on implementation. The second set of 29 such strategies was tabled in Parliament in February 2001 for the period 2001-2003. The strategies are developed in consultation with stakeholders, and articulate sustainable development goals and detailed action plans. The Commissioner of the Environment and Sustainable Development reports to Parliament on the implementation of the strategies.

At the provincial level, Manitoba has prepared 11 sectoral sustainable development strategies to guide policy, and Alberta has created an inter-ministerial Sustainable Development Co-ordinating Council. In 1998, the Quebec Government established a strategy for economic development that is based in part on sustainable development principles.

> ### Manitoba's *Sustainable Development Act*, 1998
>
> - establishes the Manitoba Round Table for Sustainable Development for the purpose of promoting sustainable development in Manitoba and providing advice and recommendations to government;
> - establishes the principles and guidelines of sustainable development;
> - requires the government to have in place a Sustainable Development Strategy for Manitoba;
> - provides for the preparation of component strategies whose purpose is to set out strategic plans for achieving sustainability in specific economic, environmental, resource, human health and social policy sectors;
> - requires the government to adopt sustainability indicators and prepare a Provincial Sustainability Report based on the indicators every five years;
> - requires the government to establish a provincial sustainable development code of practice for the public sector;
> - requires the government to establish financial management guidelines for evaluating the sustainability of public sector activities;
> - requires the government to establish sustainable development procurement guidelines and public sector procurement goals;
> - requires annual reporting of progress by government departments;
> - requires Crown corporations to adopt and implement financial management and procurement guidelines;
> - requires the adoption of a financial management and procurement guideline regulation to govern local government(s), school divisions, universities, colleges and regional health authorities;
> - provides the minister with the authority to: direct a public sector organization to undertake a review of its progress at implementing sustainable development; or, request the Provincial Auditor to undertake a review with the report being tabled in the legislature.

e) Economic incentives

Canadian governments have made few attempts to systematically use economic instruments to promote the integration of environmental considerations into economic decision-making, although several examples of such instruments exist (examples are: deposit refund schemes for beverage containers in several provinces; improved federal tax treatment for the donation of ecologically-valuable lands; Ozone-Depleting Substances Regulations under the *Canadian Environmental Protection Act (CEPA)*, which is a tradable regime; tax credits and accelerated depreciation for certain energy technologies; Nova Scotia tax credits to companies receiving ISO 14001 certification). Both Ontario and the federal government have also introduced limited emissions trading schemes to improve the efficiency of environmental protection, and industry-non-government organization coalitions in Ontario and Alberta are working to promote trading regimes for air pollutants. In this respect, Canada's approach to sustainable development stands in contrast to that of several Organization for Economic Co-operation and Development (OECD) countries that have made much greater use of economic instruments.

Over the 1990s, several Canadian governments reduced program spending, including subsidies to various economic activities, largely as part of their deficit-cutting efforts. Where these subsidies had environmentally perverse effects (such as subsidies to energy mega-projects), the cuts have reduced the pressure on environmental resources. Many environmentalists argue that it is inappropriate that several government programs continue to encourage resource development at the expense of the environment.

It is difficult to comment on the overall impact of these government initiatives. While changes to decision-making practices are essential if government policies are to promote more sustainable forms of development, their impact is both indirect and long-term: they do not translate into immediate changes in environmental, social or economic conditions and their effects are not always apparent. Nevertheless, the steps that Canadian governments have taken over the last decade allow a more systematic consideration of environmental values in decision-making and increase consultation, transparency and public accountability.

"The sense of "immensity" and Canada's rich endowment of natural resources have led to policies favouring their development and use...Support has been especially important for activities based on non-renewable resources (such as oil, gas, metals and minerals), coming mostly in the form of preferential tax treatment. Although the recently-announced tax measures will, over time, contribute to leveling the playing field, this has put other sectors of the economy ... at a disadvantage.... The resulting intensive exploitation of non-renewable resources also has environmental consequences in the form of polluting substance release and greenhouse gas emissions."

**Economic Survey of Canada, 2000
Organisation for Economic Co-operation and Development**

While the federal, provincial and territorial governments were implementing these reforms, many were also cutting their environmental and natural resource management budgets as part of an overall effort to control their deficits. In some cases these cuts reduced government capacity to conduct scientific research, develop new programs and enforce environmental regulations. In his 2000-2001 Annual Report, the Environmental Commissioner of Ontario, the province with the largest population and biggest economy, noted that:

between 1996 and 2000, MOE [Ministry of the Environment of the Province of Ontario] decreased ministry-initiated inspections by 34 per cent. This corresponded with a 25 per cent reduction in Operations staff responsible for inspections and abatement work during the same period. In addition, MOE also cut the number of staff and resources available to

MOE's Legal Services Branch and at MOE's Laboratory Services Branch. As noted below, these branches also play important roles in MOE's enforcement and compliance activities.

While some governments have begun to reinvest in focused environmental programs, Canadian environmental groups continue to demand that governments restore environmental budgets to their previous levels. In January 2002, a judicial inquiry concluded that budget cuts to the Ontario Ministry of the Environment "made it less likely" that government monitoring could have prevented the deaths of seven and the illness of 2300 people from contaminated water in Walkerton, Ontario.

While provincial spending on pollution abatement and control increased rapidly in the late 1980s and early 1990s, it dropped off in the mid-1990s (no figures are available after 1996). Federal spending, on the other hand, increased in the mid-90s before leveling off. In Canada, it is municipal governments that spend the most on pollution abatement and control, in large part because of heavy infrastructure commitments (on sewage disposal and waste collection).

Figure 2.1: Government Expenditures on Pollution Abatement and Control

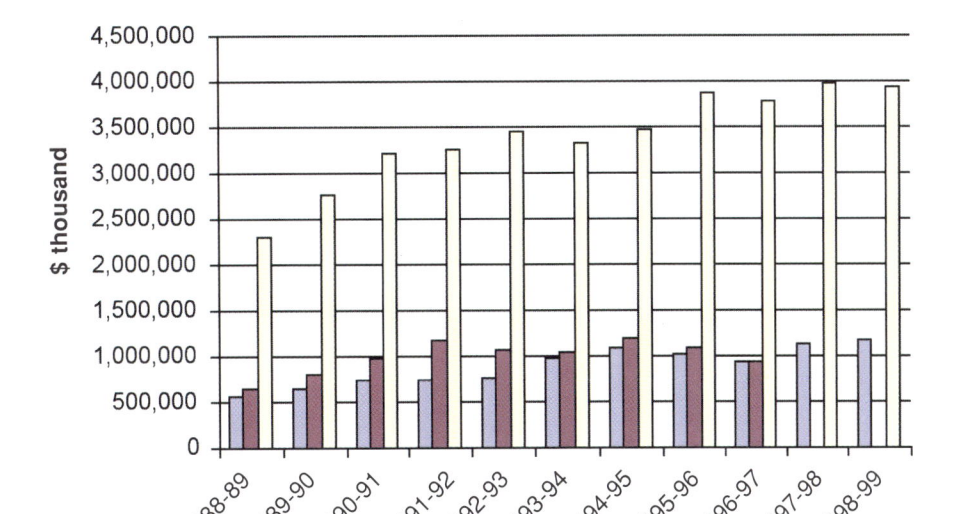

Source: Statistics Canada (2000) *Human Activity and the Environment.*

Changes to Decision-Making Structures and Processes

Sustainable Development: A Canadian Perspective

2.2 CORPORATE INITIATIVES

Over the past decade, the business sector came to play a bigger role in Canadian environmental policy, as many companies recognized the value of a proactive approach to environmental management and governments searched for new models to respond to the limits of purely regulatory approaches and more stringent budgetary constraints. Since the early 1990s, Canadian corporations have applied diverse and at times highly innovative approaches to address environmental protection, broader issues of corporate social responsibility and stakeholder engagement. As a generalization, large companies have had greater resources, and usually more incentives, to factor environmental and social considerations into their operations than small and medium enterprises (SMEs). Nevertheless, many SMEs have played their part in advancing a sustainable development agenda. For example, there have been advancements where such enterprises are part of coordinated supply chain or industrial park initiatives, or where they have participated in research and innovation in sustainable goods and services.

Over the past decade, many Canadian companies have become more engaged with practices that better contribute to sustainable development as a result of many different factors such as increased competition from trade liberalization; the democratization of information through advances in information technology; pressures from stakeholder communities to be more transparent about financial, economic, environmental and social performance; marketplace opportunities; greater consumer demands; and increasing interest by capital markets in the relationship among environmental, social and financial performance. At the same time as Canadian companies were adapting to new pressures and opportunities, the federal and some provincial governments were signaling their interest in promoting voluntary non-regulatory measures to environmental protection through more collaborative, industry-government partnerships.

The 1990s, therefore, saw a substantial increase in corporate environmental and social engagement through which companies have seen opportunities to:

- Minimize risk and liability by:
    - adopting certified environmental management systems and risk control practices,
    - keeping ahead of, and influencing, regulatory practice by moving from 'compliance' to 'beyond compliance,'
    - contributing to the maintenance of healthy and viable communities, in order to protect the "social license to operate," and
    - addressing stakeholder expectations regarding openness, transparency and accountability.

- Create value for investors and other stakeholders by:
  - developing innovative products and services with demonstrable environmental and social benefits and financial returns,
  - aligning the interests of investors with those of society at large, for example through socially responsible investment, and
  - enhancing access to financial capital in the equity markets, debt financing and credit.

While this emerging "business case" for sustainable development has not yet been adopted widely across Canadian industry, there has been substantial progress and evidence of strong leadership on corporate social responsibility in a number of industrial sectors.

This involvement has manifested itself in activities such as:

- *Beyond-compliance initiatives:* A number of Canadian companies have shifted from an orientation based on compliance and 'environment as a cost' to one that focuses on 'environment as value creation.' They have introduced cleaner forms of production, improved their eco-efficiency, and have begun to manage some of their products on a life-cycle basis. The greater attention paid to environmental factors is particularly evident in the areas of toxic chemicals and improved energy efficiency (see chapters 5 and 8).

> "BC Hydro has adopted sustainability as the driving force of our business... We are serious about achieving an optimum balance of environmental, economic and social considerations in everything we do, because it's the right thing to do. The journey towards sustainability is good for business, for people and for the planet."
>
> **BC Hydro, Triple Bottom Line Report, 2001**

- *Adoption of "triple-bottom line" strategies:* A number of companies have started to develop more integrated corporate strategies to address environmental, social and economic needs. The most advanced are integrating triple bottom line factors into corporate decision-making and addressing the needs of their stakeholders while also increasing shareholder value.

- *Testing the use of market instruments:* More and more companies are engaging in pilot projects to test market instruments such as emissions trading to reduce pollution. Early actors are assessing the environmental, economic and social benefits and opportunities that exist with these market transformation initiatives.

> "...we have come to appreciate the challenges a sustainable energy future presents – a challenge that involves working to improve our environmental, economic and social performance, while resolving what initially appears to be conflicting stakeholder interests and expectations.
>
> **Rick George, President**
> **Suncor Energy Inc.**

Changes to Decision-Making Structures and Processes

- *Voluntary codes of conduct:* A small number of industry sectors have adopted voluntary environmental codes of conduct as a condition to membership in the industry association, and others are considering similar initiatives. The Canadian Chemical Producers' Association began developing its Responsible Care© program (now adapted in over 40 countries) in the mid-1980s and has inspired similar initiatives in other sectors such as the Environmental Commitment and Responsibility program of the Canadian Electricity Association. The forest products, mining, steel and petroleum industries have also adopted environmental policies to which their member companies are expected to adhere, and in some cases, have established guidelines to promote best practices.
- *Public consultation:* Stakeholder engagement has become an increasingly important aspect of business for many companies, especially in the resource-extraction industry and more particularly at the community level. Further, a growing number of Canadian companies (26 out of Canada's 100 largest companies) are reporting publicly on their sustainable development performance and practices.
- *Participation in government-sponsored challenge programs:* The Voluntary Challenge Registry (VCR) to reduce greenhouse gas emissions (GHGs) and the Accelerated Reduction/Elimination of Toxics Program (ARET) have been an important aspect of corporate environmental activity in Canada, particularly with regard to controlling emissions of GHGs and toxic substances. In addition, several companies and industry associations have negotiated pollution prevention agreements with governments. In Alberta, the Clean Air Strategic Alliance is a unique multi-stakeholder partnership for managing air quality issues. Participating businesses view recognition of corporate performance by these programs as an opportunity to demonstrate to key stakeholders their commitment to address important environmental issues.
- *Pursuit of the strategic 'value proposition' of sustainability:* A number of Canada's leading companies have been selected to the Dow Jones Sustainability Index and other stock market indices that promote the link between social and environmental performance, and stock price performance.

> *"When Dofasco makes a decision or takes an action, we strive to be mindful of the implications for the broader community and for the next generation. At Dofasco, we have seen first-hand the long-term correlation between financial, environmental and social factors in defining success of a company and a community."*
>
> **John Mayberry, President**
> **Dofasco Inc. 2000 Annual Report**

While Canadian environmental non-government organizations have welcomed corporate initiatives to improve their environmental performance, many have also strongly criticized the effectiveness of some government-sponsored challenge programs (ARET, VCR).

The environmental community has advocated for some time that the Minister of the Environment develop and adopt more rigorous requirements for managing voluntary initiatives. In 1999, the Commissioner of the Environment and Sustainable Development made a similar recommendation. In response to these concerns, Environment Canada issued its Environmental Performance Agreement Policy in June 2001, outlining essential principles (credibility, accountability and cost-effectiveness). Through this policy, Environment Canada promotes voluntary initiatives with the private sector and has established greater incentives for stakeholder participation. The Canadian Chemical Producers' Association, Environment Canada, Health Canada, Industry Canada, Alberta, Ontario and Saskatchewan have since signed the first environmental performance agreement to reduce pollution from chemical production.

2.3 Non-Governmental Organizations

Non-government organizations (NGOs) – not-for-profit organizations such as church groups, labour unions, environmental organizations, consumer groups, development groups, social welfare organizations and youth groups – have a significant role in the Canadian sustainable development agenda. NGOs enjoy high public credibility and play an essential role in Canadian society in raising awareness, pressing for change and holding governments accountable. There are five categories of actions by Canadian NGOs in support of sustainable development since Rio:

a) *Working for on-the-ground change, primarily locally, but also internationally:* NGOs have initiated and helped implement programs to increase public awareness of environmental and social issues, change consumer lifestyles and implement specific policy reforms such as energy and water efficiency, improved urban transit, protection of local landscapes, and help for the disadvantaged.

b) *Participating in the ongoing U.N. negotiating processes developed to carry Rio work forward:* Canadian NGOs have been involved in various international negotiation and implementation processes on climate change, biodiversity, persistent organic pollutants (POPs), social development, women's and children's rights.

c) *Pressing for change through advocacy, based on research and grassroots organizing:* The Sierra Club of Canada, for example, coordinated a Rio Watch process, engaging the support of 80 other groups in the ongoing tracking of progress by governments. The World Wildlife Fund of Canada led a decade-long campaign to increase the number of protected areas in Canada (see chapter 6). A Green Budget Coalition, consisting of 15 leading national environmental groups, has been pressing for ecological fiscal reform by making detailed proposals for inclusion in the federal government's annual budget. A broad coalition of Canadian NGOs led the opposition to the OECD's proposed Multilateral Agreement on Investment. The 1996 eco-summit held by l'Union québécoise pour la conservation de la nature and several other NGOs attracted 5000 participants and launched 500 sustainable development projects in every region of Quebec.

d) *Advocating changes through coalitions with the private sector:* As well as working with government and other parts of civil society, NGOs are also forging coalitions with the private sector (such as the Species at Risk Working Group, Clean Air Renewable Energy Coalition) and discussion forums such as the New Directions Group. Various interest groups are seeking common ground on some of the more pressing environmental and social issues.

e) *Partnering between Canadian and developing country NGOs and institutions:* Partnerships between Canadian and developing country NGOs and institutions are intended to meet community needs with a practical, hands-on approach to finding environmentally sound solutions; to build and strengthen the capacity of developing country partner organizations to manage environmental challenges; to contribute to poverty reduction; and to promote changes towards ecologically sustainable lifestyles.

Through these and many other actions, Canadian civil society organizations have continued to be effective agents for change and have persistently pressed for more sustainable forms of development. In 2001, the federal government and representatives of the voluntary sector signed a framework accord agreeing to closer collaboration. This Voluntary Sector Initiative will involve joint work in knowledge and skills development, participation in policy development, information technologies, public awareness and regulatory issues.

> *"While governments may tire of criticism from civil society for the failure to meet UNCED promises, many understand the reality that NGO pressure is essential. Without a chorus of voices reminding the media and the public of the urgent nature of the threats, Cabinet colleagues would also be unlikely to support moving to the Rio goals."*
>
> **Elizabeth May, Executive Director Sierra Club of Canada**

2.4 LABOUR

The Canadian labour movement has been active on various aspects of the sustainable development agenda, through policy formulation and advocacy, training of workers, and efforts to integrate health and safety and other sustainability issues into contracts. The

Canadian Labour Congress, for example, has involved itself in issues ranging from pesticide use to species protection to the creation of green jobs. It has worked to assist its member unions to incorporate employee health and safety safeguards into collective agreements. As well, it has followed a proactive social agenda addressing such domestic issues as the status of social programs, and such international issues as racism.

At the provincial level, the Quebec-based Confederation of National Trade Unions developed a statement of environmental principles in 1993, and since then has been working to incorporate environmental clauses into collective agreements. It also has implemented training programs for its members on sustainable development, and more specifically on the ISO 14001 environmental management system standard.

2.5 Education for Sustainable Development

In 1992, shortly after UNCED, over 4000 environmental educators from 90 countries came together in Toronto for the largest gathering of environmental educators in Canadian history, Eco-Ed. Canada has engaged its citizens to learn about their environment through initiatives such as the Canadian Network for Environmental Education and Communication (EECOM), established in 1993. EECOM's mission is to engage Canadians in learning about their environment by enabling teachers, educators, and communicators to work together to nurture environmentally-informed and responsible individuals, organizations and communities.

At the post-secondary level, the Canadian Consortium for Sustainable Development Research (CCSDR) brings together research institutes and major teaching programs in the areas of sustainable development, environmental policy and environmental technology. The network includes the heads of the major environmental studies programs teaching at the graduate level and university-based research centres and institutes. Several Canadian universities (such as British Columbia, Moncton, New Brunswick, Ecole Polytechnique, l'Université du Québec à Montréal, Sherbrooke) have established Chairs, Centres or Institutes in Sustainable Development. The Quebec government has created a 'Fonds d'action québécois pour le développement durable' to finance research and provide student grants. For its part, the federal government established scholarships to promote inter-disciplinary research on issues related to sustainable development.

Other noteworthy education initiatives include:
- Learning for a Sustainable Future (LSF), a not-for-profit organization that works with educators from across Canada to integrate the concepts and principles of sustainable development into curricula at all grade levels, through support for sustainability

curriculum and policy development, materials development, professional development, and capacity building.
- The Hurley Island Project, an Internet-based sustainability education and technology course that gathers secondary students from across Canada in the same virtual classroom to exchange visions of a sustainable future for Canada.
- Green Street, an innovative pilot project in Atlantic Canada, Alberta and British Columbia, makes it easier for teachers and students to choose a pre-screened environmental program to meet their needs and interests.
- FEESA, an Environmental Education Society in Alberta, promotes, coordinates and supports bias-balanced environmental and sustainability education on issues such as energy, climate change, and water.
- The Nova Scotia Museum of Natural History phenology project Thousand Eyes, where students observe, record, and study natural history events with a view to understanding climate change. This project is based on an observation initiative undertaken in Nova Scotia schools one hundred years ago.

Some of the most important environmental education occurs outside the classroom. Governments continue to play an important role in providing consumers with information about the environmental implications of the choices they make by, for instance, publishing energy efficiency ratings for automobiles and appliances. Many utilities publish advice on how to reduce energy and water consumption. For their part, environmental groups have made the raising of public environmental awareness the cornerstone of their activities, and organize a variety of activities on specific issues such as wildlife conservation, clean air and the reduced use of pesticides.

Since 1999, Environment Canada has engaged over 5,400 Canadians in a nation-wide consultation with a view to developing a *National Framework for Environment Learning and Sustainability*. This is Canada's response to UNESCO's request that nations implement the recommendations contained in Chapter 36 of *Agenda 21: Promoting Education, Public Awareness and Training*. The Framework, along with over 300 action plans from members of a strategic alliance on education and sustainability from all sectors of society, will be tabled at the World Summit on Sustainable Development (WSSD) in 2002.

By definition, educational efforts take time to bear fruit. While Canadians are more environmentally-aware than ever before, polling research also reveals that many do not make the link between their lifestyle choices and environmental effects. This has led to inconsistent behaviours, such as high rates of household recycling co-existing with a continued demand for large gas-guzzling vehicles.

2.6 Continuing Challenges

Making sustainable development a reality is a long term process. The measures that governments have taken over the last decade help integrate environmental factors into policies and programs. Continuing challenges remain, including jurisdictional fragmentation, incomplete environmental information, competing priorities and the lack of agreed metrics. Incorporating sustainable development considerations into industrial policy in order to promote the link among innovation, environmental performance and competitiveness will require cutting across traditional policy processes and structures. In the business sector, the challenge remains to involve a large number of companies of all sizes into triple bottom line decision-making and building a business case for practices and products that go beyond eco-efficiency and towards sustainable production and consumption objectives. While civil society has more opportunities than ever before to influence government and corporate development decisions, many NGOs feel that the lack of resources constrains their ability to participate effectively. Civil society organizations also face continued challenges to increase their own accountability to the public. Ensuring that education for sustainability is infused into all provincial and territorial curricula will require further inter-jurisdictional cooperation.

3 SOCIAL SUSTAINABILITY

While the Rio Summit focused mainly on environmental protection and economic development, Agenda 21 did address several commonly accepted elements of social sustainability including poverty, demographics, human health and human settlements. UNCED was also followed by a series of social development summits and related conferences in which Canada played a proactive role, and made important commitments to improve social conditions domestically and to support improvements internationally. The latter element is addressed in Chapter 10.

The declarations and action plans of these various international conferences form a vast array of commitments. For the purposes of this report, the following are used as indicators of Canadian commitment to domestic follow-up:
- the goal of eradicating poverty (at the World Summit on Social Development); and
- the elimination of all forms of discrimination against women, the promotion of women's economic independence, and the eradication of the burden of poverty on women (at the Beijing World Conference on Women).

3.1 SOCIAL INVESTMENT

If countries around the world have made progress in the decade since Rio in defining environmental and economic sustainability, they have found it more difficult to define social sustainability. According to one measure of social development – the United Nations Development Program's Human Development Index (HDI), that integrates health, education and income – Canada has fared very well during the 1990s, ranking first in the world for six consecutive years between 1995 to 2000, and third in 2001.

Investment in human capital, and in particular in health and education, is one important measure of progress in social sustainability. In Canada, the provinces deliver most of the important social programs (health, education, social assistance, basic income support, child care, worker training, etc.). The federal government provides financial support to the provinces to ensure that these programs are broadly comparable across the country.

The federal government cut transfer payments to the provinces in the mid-1990s in an effort to reduce mounting deficits. Some provincial governments cut their social spending for the same reason. Since that time, the federal government has reinvested in social programs through increases to the Canada Health and Social Transfer (CHST) to provinces and territories and through the creation of the federal/provincial/territorial National Child Benefit initiative in 1998. Federal transfers do not require provincial and territorial social programs to meet national standards. In exchange for receiving CHST payments, provinces must adhere to the principles of the Canada Health Act and are required to provide social assistance without minimum residency requirements.

In Canada, as in many other OECD countries, health spending represents a substantial portion of government expenditures and has been consuming an increasing proportion of government budgets over the 1990s. Canadians have one of the highest levels of life expectancy in the world, two years higher than in the United States. Observers give part of the credit to the success of health care programs that provide universal coverage for most needed services.

Canada's aging population and increased costs of treatment (such as pharmaceutical drugs, new technologies, increasing salaries of medical staff) have put growing financial pressures on the health care system. Total health spending has, however, remained fairly constant as a share of GDP in the 1990s, mainly because of government cuts in the mid- to late-1990s followed by increases over the past two years. The private portion of health care costs has grown somewhat because government programs do not cover drug costs, dental treatment and some long-term care (except for the elderly and for the very poor). The large share of total government budgets consumed by health costs has resulted in some attempts to cut costs, and an ongoing national debate on which services should continue to be provided free of charge.

Education spending in Canada dropped relative to GDP over much of the 1990s although it increased in absolute terms, reflecting in part the declining share of youth in the Canadian population. Over this period, most provincial governments shifted a portion of the costs of post-secondary education to students by increasing tuition fees, resulting in a public debate regarding equitable access to education. Canada, nevertheless, has one of the highest post-secondary education enrollment rates in the world.

3.2 Budgetary Measures

Government action in the early and mid-1990s, to address Canada's fiscal problems by eliminating government deficits, established a foundation for real income growth in the latter part of the 1990s. Average family incomes hit new highs at the end of the 1990s after a rebound from the recession in the early 1990s. While real after-tax income fell by 4.8 per cent from 1990 to 1993, it grew by 8.6 per cent from 1993 to 1999.

In addition to income growth, prudent fiscal management in the 1990s has allowed the federal and provincial governments to balance their budgets, and for the federal and several provincial governments in Alberta, Ontario and British Columbia to introduce significant tax reductions.

For example, in 2000, the federal government introduced a tax reduction plan that is expected to provide $100 billion in cumulative tax relief by 2004-05. Of this tax relief, over $81 billion will accrue to individuals, with about 60 per cent going to help low- and middle-income Canadians. By 2004-05, the federal government's tax reduction plan is expected to reduce the personal income tax burden of all Canadians by 21 per cent on average, and by 27 per cent for families with children.

3.3 Eradicating Poverty

Unlike other countries, Canada does not have an official definition of poverty. A "basic needs" approach, such as that used by the World Bank to define extreme poverty (US$1 per person per day) is inappropriate in rich, industrial countries such as Canada, where virtually everybody has a higher income. In consultation with the provinces and the territories, the federal government is proposing a measure of poverty based on the minimum income that a household would need to meet its needs, taking into account prevailing community standards.

Applying a measure of poverty similar to that used by the United Nations (less than one half of median income), 11.5 per cent of the Canadian population lived in poor households in 1999. This percentage is down from 12.0 per cent in 1996, but up from the all-time low of 10.2 per cent in 1989. On the basis of this measure, Canada has significantly less poverty than the United States (16 per cent) but double the rate found in Scandinavian countries (5 per cent).

The growth in average incomes in the latter part of the 1990s has contributed to a lower incidence of low incomes in Canada. This growth, however, has also coincided with an increase in market income disparity over the period. In 1989, the top 20 per cent of families received 41.9 per cent of total market income; in 1999 this figure stood at 44.4 per cent. At the same time, the share of income going to the 20 per cent of families with the lowest income decreased from 3.8 per cent to 3.5 per cent.

Progressive income taxes and government income transfers substantially reduce income inequality. Income security programs such as Employment Insurance, benefits for seniors (including Canada Pension Plan retirement benefits, Old Age Security, and the Guaranteed Income Supplement), provincial social assistance, and benefits delivered through the tax system such as the Canada Child Tax Benefit have played an important role in offsetting the effects of low wages or insecure work, and accounted for 57 per cent of the average total income of low-income Canadians in 1999. Through the Canada Child Tax Benefit, the federal government provides financial assistance directly to Canadian families with children. Since 1998 the federal government has increased a supplement to the Canada Child Tax Benefit for low-income families with children. In total, by 2004, the government will provide about

$8 billion per year to 90 per cent of all Canadian families with children through the Canada Child Tax Benefit and the supplement.

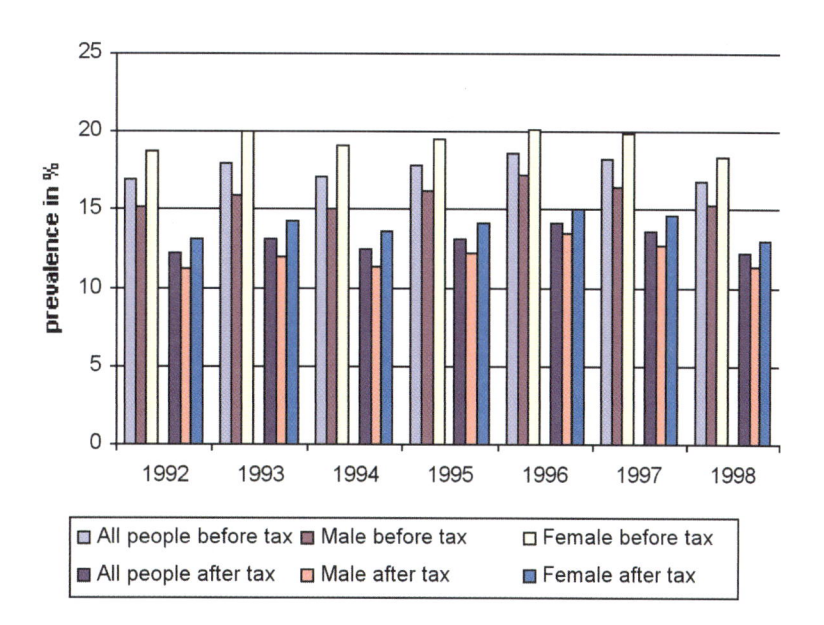

Figure 3.1: People Living in Poverty Before and After Tax

The composition of the lowest income groups has changed significantly over time. The improvement in the circumstances of senior citizens has been particularly remarkable. Twenty years ago, the elderly accounted for 10.8 per cent of the low-income population. By 1997, this percentage had fallen to 2.7 per cent. Meanwhile, the working-age share (age 18-64) of the low-income population rose from 52.4 per cent to 64.5 per cent. The retirement income system has provided Canada with substantial successes over the last few decades. The OECD has rated Canada's retirement income system as one of the best in the world in terms of equity, level of benefits and affordability.

Persons with disabilities, working families with children headed by young parents (particularly those with limited skills) and recent immigrants are more likely to be poor than other Canadians. Female single parents (43.0 per cent) and unattached non-elderly women (30.0 per cent) have very high incidences of low income. There are also significant disparities between the income of Aboriginal people and other Canadians. Canadians living in the eastern Atlantic provinces earn less income than their counterparts in other provinces. (Canadians in Alberta, British Columbia and Ontario earn the highest incomes on average).

Social Sustainability

> In 1999, the federal government announced its *Homelessness Initiative* of $753-million over three years. This Initiative engages all levels of government and community partners in the development of appropriate responses to priorities identified at the local level, including funding enhancements to existing programs. *The National Homelessness Initiative* is enhancing existing programs and developing the *Supporting Communities Partnership Initiative*, allowing communities to plan and implement comprehensive local strategies to reduce and prevent homelessness.

3.4 REGIONAL EQUITY

The persistence of large regional disparities creates major problems for the management of economic policy in a federation such as Canada. The federal government has, over the last several decades, set up a number of programs for inter-regional income distribution. Such transfers are designed to ensure that all Canadians receive reasonably comparable levels of public services, wherever they live. The federal government provides the large majority of its transfers to provinces and territories through three major programs:

- The Equalization program purpose is to ensure that less prosperous provinces have sufficient revenue to provide reasonably comparable levels of public service at reasonably comparable levels of taxation.
- Territorial formula financing allows the three territorial governments to provide services to their residents while recognizing the higher costs in the North.
- The Canada Health and Social transfer assists provincial and territorial programs in health, post-secondary education, social assistance, social services and early childhood development.

In 2001, financial transfers from the federal government to the provinces and territories are expected to total over $25 billion, accounting for 17 per cent of aggregate provincial and territorial revenue, and amounting to approximately $840 per person.

There has been significant progress over the past three decades in reducing inter-provincial disparities in per capita disposable income (PDI). In 1970, PDI in the highest-income province was 1.74 times what it was in the lowest income province. By 2000, this ratio has fallen to 1.33.

3.5 GENDER EQUITY

Today, more married women and women with children are employed in the paid labour force in Canada than ever before. While men's contribution to unpaid work has been increasing, women continue to shoulder primary responsibility for child rearing and the general care of the family and household. Women continue to spend approximately twice as much time doing unpaid work as men. This may preclude or limit women's participation in the labour market and therefore may restrict their earnings potential and financial security. In 1997, 43 per cent of female lone-parent families had income below the post-tax Low Income Measure. This was down from 49.7 per cent a decade earlier.

In 1999, women working full-time for a full year earned 69.9 per cent as much as men working full-time for a full year. Women's earnings are also affected by the fact that they are much more likely to be working part-time. However, earnings differences between women and men have been shrinking, partly because male earnings have been flat or falling, and partly because women are more highly educated and are less likely than in the past to take long leaves from the paid work force to raise children. Wage differences are smallest between highly educated young men and women, and university enrolment rates are now significantly higher among young women than young men.

3.6 Aboriginal People

Overall, Aboriginal people are worse off than non-Aboriginal people in this country, and the former Auditor-General in his end-of-term report noted "that improvements in the life of First Nations is proceeding at a frustratingly slow pace." The average annual income for Aboriginal people is half that of non-Aboriginal people, 50 per cent of Aboriginal children live in poverty, the unemployment rate is three times higher, in some places reaching as high as 90 per cent. Infant mortality is two times higher. The death rate for First Nations' infants from injury, poisoning and violence is five times higher; rates of tuberculosis are six times the national average; and life expectancy for First Nations people is seven to eight years less than the national average.

The rates of suicide, drug abuse, fetal alcohol syndrome, and HIV/AIDS are all significantly higher than for the Canadian population as a whole. High school graduation is half that of the non-Aboriginal population, as is the rate of college and university graduation. While the federal government has invested in new infrastructure to improve basic living conditions and the overall health of community members, it will take a long time to bring the conditions in Aboriginal reserves to the national average.

Social Sustainability

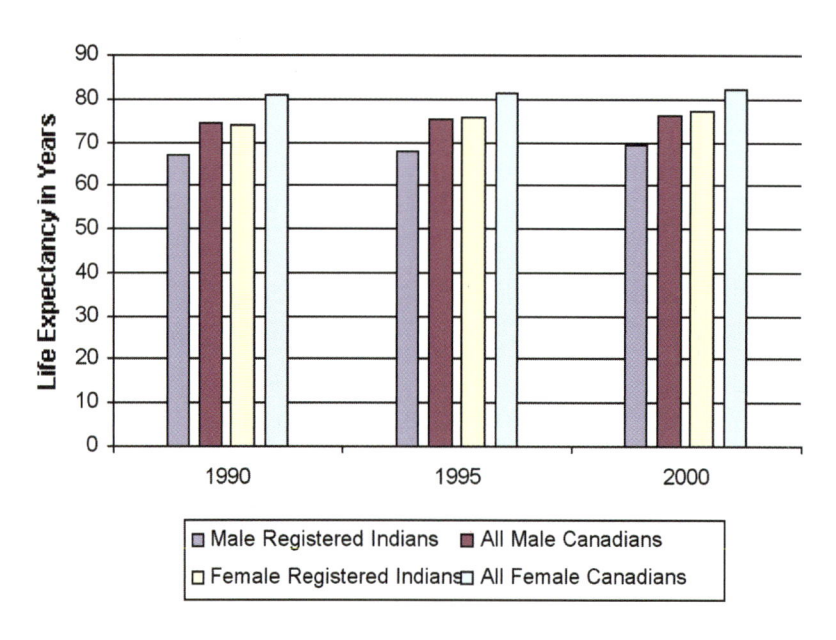

Figure 3.2: Aboriginal Life Expectancy at Birth

In recognition of the difficult past that Aboriginal people experienced when dealing with the actions of governments, and the many social and economic problems they were facing, the federal government in 1991 launched a Royal Commission on Aboriginal Peoples. After an extensive cross-country investigation, the Commissioners concluded that fundamental change is needed in the relationship between Aboriginal and non-Aboriginal people in Canada. The Royal Commission's vision included rebuilding Aboriginal nationhood; supporting effective and accountable Aboriginal governments; establishing government-to-government relationships between Canada and Aboriginal nations; and taking practical steps to improve the living conditions of Aboriginal people. It called for a partnership based on the principles of mutual respect and recognition, responsibility and sharing.

"Successive governments have tried – sometimes intentionally, sometimes in ignorance–to absorb Aboriginal people into Canadian society, thus eliminating them as distinct peoples. Policies pursued over the decades have undermined – and almost erased – Aboriginal cultures and identities. This is assimilation. It is a denial of the principles of peace, harmony and justice for which this country stands – and it has failed. Aboriginal peoples remain proudly different.

> *Assimilation policies have done great damage, leaving a legacy of brokenness affecting Aboriginal individuals, families and communities. The damage has been equally serious to the spirit of Canada – the spirit of generosity and mutual accommodation in which Canadians take pride.*
>
> *Yet the damage is not beyond repair. The key is to reverse the assumptions of assimilation that still shape and constrain Aboriginal life chances – despite some worthy reforms in the administration of Aboriginal affairs."*
>
> **Royal Commission on Aboriginal Peoples**

In 1998, the federal government responded to the Royal Commission report with a long-term, broad-based policy approach (*Gathering Strength* – Canada's Aboriginal Action Plan) designed to increase the quality of life of Aboriginal people and promote self-sufficiency. With the introduction of this plan, the federal government formally apologized for the role it played in the development and administration of Aboriginal residential schools, and is supporting efforts to address the debilitating legacy of physical, sexual, and emotional abuse suffered by Aboriginal children in these schools.

A process of change is underway to address other key dimensions of the relationship between the Government of Canada and Aboriginal people. Some progress has been made, for example, in improving housing conditions in First Nations communities. Over the past five years, the total number of houses on reserve has increased by more than 13 per cent. During the same period, there has been a significant increase in the number of houses considered to be in adequate condition.

Efforts in education reform are another example that will affect more than 110,000 First Nations students across the country. Since the Government of Canada transferred substantial control of education to First Nations, there has been considerable growth in the number of First Nations students in post-secondary programs. From 1988 to 1998, the number of Aboriginal students enrolled in post-secondary education has doubled.

Notwithstanding this progress, Aboriginal people remain deeply frustrated by the slow pace of improvement in their situation. In his report to Parliament, a former Auditor General of Canada noted that:
- In 1991, 92 per cent of claims made in the preceding 20 years had not been settled;
- As of 1996, it would take Indian students on reserves 23 years to reach education parity with the overall Canadian rate of high school completion;

Social Sustainability

- In 1998, it was not uncommon for the settling of comprehensive land claims to take more than 20 years.

Aboriginal land claims and other claims against the federal government have troubled both parties for decades. The numerous complexities of claim settlement carry wide-ranging effects that extend beyond the participants. Aboriginal people continue to be frustrated by the slow pace of settling claims.

The federal government is currently negotiating at 83 self-government tables, 70 comprehensive claims (land and self-government) tables, 92 specific claims tables and 20 treaty tables. While 16 specific claims were settled in 1999-2000, there remain Aboriginal claims to huge areas of Canada. The Métis are seeking full recognition of their rights and related issues are before the courts. However, a recent agreement with Saskatchewan is promising.

Self-government negotiations may cover areas such as education, language and culture, police services, health care and social services, housing, property rights, the enforcement of Aboriginal laws and adoption and child welfare. Through these negotiations, Aboriginal groups will shape their own forms of government to suit their particular historical, cultural, political and economic circumstances.

Issues related to land remain the most intractable. The existing historic treaties cover everything from agreements to live in peace and friendship, surrenders of Aboriginal lands, health care and education. Modern treaties generally address land claims and self-government arrangements. Most land claims agreements recognize Aboriginal environmental management regimes, or establish co-management regimes between Aboriginal and non-Aboriginal people.

While recent treaties such as the Nisga'a treaty in British Columbia, or the Inuvialuit Final Agreement in the Western Arctic, have settled large land claims by these peoples, many more remain outstanding. These include Comprehensive Claims in areas where the Aboriginal people continue to claim Aboriginal title, and specific land claims relating alleged breaches of Treaty entitlement or lawful obligation for management of land and assets.

Most First Nations people live on land set aside for them by the federal government either through legislative enactment or through historic treaties that were negotiated as Canada was being settled. Title to these lands, known as 'reserve lands,' is held by the federal government in trust for the First Nations. Many of these reserves are small isolated plots of land, with limited economic opportunities. In many cases, modern treaties and the settlement of the terms of historic treaties, will provide enhanced opportunity for economic development. The Inuit have concluded modern treaties with the federal government and have recognized land and self-government rights. The understanding and recognition of Métis rights are evolving.

Environmental protection and management are significant challenges facing indigenous communities, given that they generally do not have recognized jurisdiction to manage resources on their traditional territories. Aboriginal people are among the first to be affected by environmental degradation and in particular, their traditional diet has suffered. In many cases, the loss of traditional or 'country' food sources has resulted in a rise in disease such as diabetes, and a decline in traditional activities and culture, further undermining social conditions. While these challenges remain, seminal court cases and claims agreements (such as the Nisga'a in British Columbia) have increased statutory recognition of the rights of First Nations to manage and co-manage resources.

Land Claim And Self-Government Agreements With Aboriginal Peoples

- 2002 - The Ta'an Kwach'an Council Final Agreement
- 1999 - Nisga'a Final Agreement
- 1998 - Tr'ondëk Hwëch'in Final Agreement
- 1997 - Little Salmon/Carmacks Final Agreement
- 1997 - Selkirk First Nation Final Agreement
- 1995 - Vuntut Gwitchin First Nation Final Agreement
- 1995 - Champagne and Aishihik First Nations Final Agreement
- 1995 - Teslin Tlingit Council Final Agreement
- 1995 - First Nation of Nacho Nyak Dun
- 1994 - Sahtu Dene and Métis Comprehensive Land Claim Agreement
- 1993 - Umbrella Final Agreement Council for Yukon Indians
- 1993 - Nunavut Land Claims Agreement
- 1992 - The Gwich'in Comprehensive Land Claim Agreement
- 1984 - The Inuvialuit Final Agreement
- 1978 - The Northeastern Quebec Agreement
- 1975 - James Bay and Northern Quebec Agreement and Complementary Agreements

Social Sustainability

3.7 CONTINUING CHALLENGES

Canada faces several continuing challenges related to improving equity among social groups, regions and genders. These challenges, and programs to address them have been in place for several decades. Although Canada has made progress in increasing equity within its society over recent decades, this progress has been slow in some areas. The result is that many Canadians – Aboriginal people in particular – face ongoing challenges.

4 SUSTAINABLE COMMUNITIES

Communities of all sizes, from tiny fishing villages to large towns and cities, face the issues of sustainability and the problems of maintaining quality of life while minimizing their environmental footprint. The focus of this chapter will be on major sustainability issues faced by larger cities.

4.1 URBAN COMMUNITIES

Canada is a highly urbanized country: 80 per cent of Canadians live and work in urban areas, although since the country is large, there are significant regional variations. As a result of immigration, Canadian cities are also rapidly changing. Canada's largest city, Toronto, is now one of the most multicultural cities in the world. In 2000, Toronto received over 80,000 immigrants from more than 170 countries. Over 100 languages are spoken in Toronto, and by the year 2003, foreign-born residents will comprise more than half of Toronto's population of 2.4 million people.

For the most part, Canadian cities are safe and clean. As Canada's economic engines, accounting for a substantial portion of the country's GDP, they provide the social, economic and physical infrastructure for business to develop, and for workers and families to live in secure and healthy neighbourhoods. Health care in urban centres is accessible, diverse, and of high quality. Canadian cities also provide excellent education opportunities as most of Canada's best universities and colleges are in larger urban areas.

Canadian cities, however, also face complex, interrelated challenges that are having adverse effects on quality of life and long-term sustainability. These include urban sprawl, leading to rising energy consumption, greenhouse gas emissions, and the loss of prime agricultural land (more than 10 per cent of Canada's prime agricultural land has already been converted to urban uses); pollution to air, water and land; and related health issues that affect vulnerable populations such as the young, the elderly and the sick. Other interrelated issues confronted by Canadian communities include access to affordable housing, homelessness, income disparity, the downturn of traditional industries, inadequate infrastructure, immigration to urban areas, emigration of rural youth, and a shift in the skills required for a knowledge-based economy.

Over the 1990s, Canada's metropolitan areas continued to grow by spreading into formerly rural areas. Cities within commuting distances of the large urban centres of Toronto, Montreal and Vancouver grew especially quickly. This evolving urban pattern is linked to the changing nature of manufacturing, the growing share of services in the economy and shifting retailing

Sustainable Communities

Sustainable Development: A Canadian Perspective

patterns. Manufacturing and service industries and retail centres relocate or are newly-established in the suburbs and metro-adjacent satellite communities, leading to a new "multi-nucleated urban form," particularly around Montreal and Toronto.

This pattern of growth has increased the demand for transportation services and, particularly, the private automobile. In 1992, there were 13.3 million passenger cars in operation in Canada – nearly one car for every two people, the highest rate of car ownership in the world next to the United States. In 2000, the number of cars/light trucks registered for use in Canada had increased to 16.8 million. By contrast, urban transit use remained essentially level during this same period.

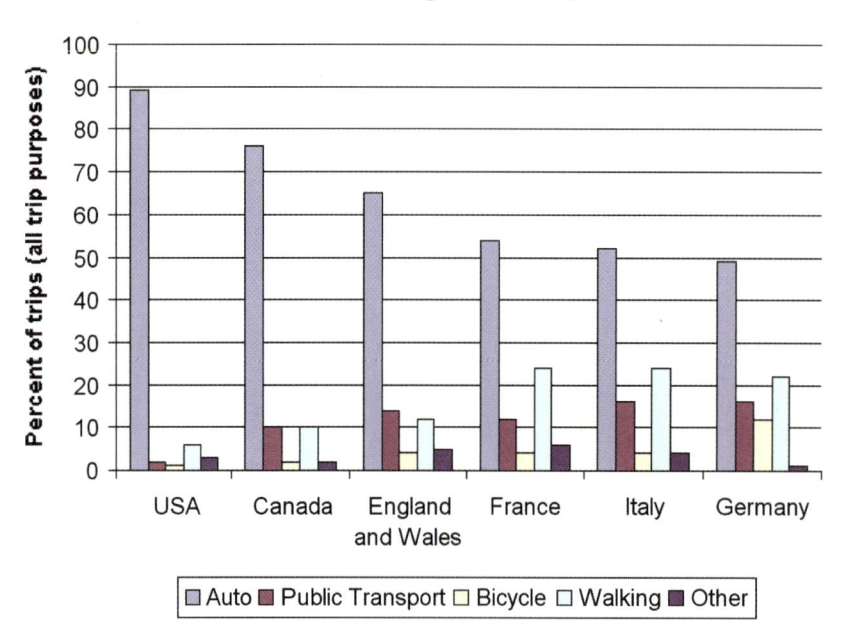

Figure 4.1: International Comparison: Modal Split for Urban Passenger Travel, 1995

Urban sprawl, traffic congestion and the ever-increasing number of cars in Canada are directly connected and all have an impact on human health and the natural environment. In Canada, transportation sources are responsible for 59 per cent of the emissions of smog-causing nitrogen oxides and 27 per cent of volatile organic compounds. Greenhouse gas emissions

> "All of us are affected by air pollution. Whether you are the Mayor of Toronto or a homeless person on the street, we all need to breathe. Since vehicles are one of the most significant sources of air pollutants in this City, we need to take bold measures to reduce our reliance on cars."
>
> **Dr. Sheela Basrur,**
> **Medical Officer of Health, Toronto**

from transportation sources, primarily cars and light trucks, account for approximately 26 per cent of the Canadian total.

According to Pollution Probe, a Canadian NGO, and the Canadian Urban Transit Association, Canadian tax law and government policies encourage inefficient, polluting automobile commuting, while discouraging efficient, cleaner public transit. These organizations calculate that transit riders in the province of Ontario pay about 75 per cent of the cost of their trip, while car drivers pay 60 per cent of the cost of their ride, with taxpayers paying the remainder through road-building and maintenance and other services. This bias has been compounded by a drop in overall transit funding of 25 per cent over the past five years.

Many municipalities are already taking action on measures to combat congestion costs and health effects of continued urban traffic growth. Most municipal master plans, particularly for larger urban centres, address traffic demand management in some form, including pedestrian/bicycle infrastructure enhancements, transit improvement and other measures to influence driving behaviour. There are also private sector and NGO initiatives, such as commute trip-reduction programs, active transportation promotion campaigns and car-sharing programs. While these initiatives all yield appreciable benefits, their scope is not broad enough to counter the trend of increasing urban car use.

Over the last decade, the federal, provincial and municipal governments have undertaken several initiatives to promote more sustainable forms of development at the municipal level, as demonstrated in the following examples:
- In the last two years, the federal government has committed $250 million to the development of two Green Municipal Funds. Managed by the Federation of Canadian Municipalities (FCM), these complementary funds are intended to encourage investment in innovative municipal projects. By leveraging investments from municipal, provincial and territorial governments, the Green Municipal Funds increase public/private partnerships and also recognize the strong role of municipalities in the promotion of sustainable development. Concurrently, the federal government committed to creating a Strategic Infrastructure Foundation, with a minimum federal commitment of $2 billion, to fund large strategic projects; and confirmed $680 million in funding for a capital grants program to alleviate the shortage of affordable housing. The Urban Transportation Showcase Program was developed to demonstrate, evaluate and promote effective strategies to reduce greenhouse gas emissions from urban transportation. This program will be delivered in partnership with the provinces and municipalities to promote effective sustainable transportation in Canadian communities.
- British Columbia is currently developing a Community Charter to enable municipalities to become more self-reliant by providing them with greater autonomy, independence, new

powers, better financial tools, and other tools for governing communities and delivering services.

- In addition, provincial and territorial governments have taken initiatives to promote more sustainable communities by managing urban growth (such as British Columbia's *Growth Strategies Act*); improving infrastructure (Saskatchewan); raising community awareness on specific environmental issues (Alberta); managing solid wastes (Nova Scotia, Quebec, Ontario); protecting water quality (Manitoba, Ontario, Quebec); and strengthening community planning (Yukon, Nova Scotia).

- Toronto is implementing an environmental plan (*Clean, Green and Healthy: A Plan for an Environmentally Sustainable Toronto*) that includes the creation of a Sustainability Round Table of stakeholders to promote environmental health, economic vitality and social equity. The Environmental Conservation and Management Strategy of the City of Ottawa provides for a governance framework that applies sustainable development planning principles to local government practices and outlines procedures for the development of municipal policies and action plans on the environment.

- Municipal governments hold many of the levers to control emissions, including land use planning, public transit and waste management. The Partners for Climate Protection (PCP) program receives funding from the federal government to bring together 90 Canadian municipalities to reduce the local production of GHG emissions and improve quality of life. The PCP offers capacity building through workshops, tools such as inventory and projection software, and data collection support.

Toronto Atmospheric Fund

The City of Toronto created the Toronto Atmospheric Fund (TAF) in 1992 with an endowment of $23 million from the sale of city property to help Toronto meet its goal of reducing GHG emissions by 20 per cent by 2005. TAF has supported a number of innovative projects including the Better Building Partnership and the Clean Air Investment Fund.

The Better Building Partnership is a successful public-private partnership that promotes and implements building renewal and energy efficiency retrofits of industrial, commercial, institutional and multi-residential buildings. TAF is one of the many partners in the project that has implemented retrofits in over 450 buildings. Through this work 3,800 person years of employment were created, $19 million was saved and carbon dioxide emissions have been reduced by 132,000 tonnes per year (City of Toronto, 2001).

In October 2001, TAF has also agreed to fund the Clean Air Investment Trust that will finance energy efficiency initiatives. These energy savings projects will improve air quality, reduce GHG emissions and reduce expenditures on energy.

- Based on public input, the City of Edmonton developed a 30-year Waste Management Strategic Plan that provides the overall framework for the ongoing development and improvement of waste management practices. Working in part with private sector partners, the implementation of the plan has enabled Edmonton to divert approximately 70 per cent of its residential waste from landfill, more than any other major Canadian city. Key components include household participation in recycling; a state-of-the-art co-composting facility, a materials recovery facility, a leachate treatment plant; landfill gas recovery; and public education programs. These programs and technologies have provided an opportunity for Edmonton to work with private sector and academic partners to develop a Waste Management Centre of Excellence with a focus on education, research, and technology.
- Nova Scotia has led the provinces in waste reduction by achieving its goal of 50 per cent waste diverted from landfill through a rigorous program of education and cooperation from industry, municipalities and the general public.

4.2 Rural Canada

Many rural Canadians face rising economic and employment challenges. High transportation costs increase the costs of most goods and services. Fewer traditional jobs in primary resource industries and downsizing, and increased centralization within all levels of government, have reduced the number of suitable employment options. Maintaining adequate services and infrastructure (health, education) becomes more difficult when young people leave rural areas in search of better economic and social opportunities.

Single industry communities that depend on the exploitation of a single natural resource such as forests, minerals, agriculture or fish face particular sustainability challenges. There are approximately 650 such communities in Canada dependent on the forest industry alone, and many more are dependent on other resource industries. While most may be geographically remote and distant from major population centres, they are intimately tied to the world economy and directly affected by swings in international commodity prices. When the resource upon which these communities depend is depleted, or becomes uneconomic, the social consequences can be profound. Several such communities have lost their economic foundation over the last decade (some mining towns in the North and some fishing communities on the East Coast), causing financial hardship, forcing re-settlement and often the loss of a way of life for the town's former inhabitants.

The unique challenges confronting such communities include the difficulties faced by farm families on the Prairies and across the country, the anxieties of Canada's mining or other single-industry towns and the loss of traditional sources of employment on both coasts. People in these communities have the same needs as urban Canadians – quality health care and education, and work that is steady and well-paying. The difference in rural and remote communities is that a hospital restructuring, a school cutback or a factory closure can have a far greater impact – perhaps even threatening the viability of the community itself.

Canada promotes an integrated approach to sustainable rural development. This cross-government, cross-sector (agriculture, forestry, natural resources, etc.) process builds partnerships with rural people and their communities to address key rural issues. For example, in 1998, the federal government launched the Canadian Rural Partnership (CRP) to better equip communities to be able to share in the benefits of the global knowledge-based economy. The CRP is an innovative, "bottom-up" approach that is aimed at coordinating government programs, policies and activities in support of rural communities, and that involves rural communities in decision-making and capacity building. A significant component of the CRP is the "rural lens" through which policies and programs of the federal government are being scrutinized to take rural considerations into account.

4.3 INTERNATIONAL INITIATIVES

Canada was among the early supporters of the development of an international framework for *Local Agenda 21*. In recognition of the critical role that local governments play in building sustainable societies, the International Development Research Centre, in cooperation with the UN Development Programme, the Netherlands Ministry of Foreign Affairs and the Toronto-based International Council for Local Environmental Initiatives (ICLEI), launched an international action research program on sustainable development planning in 1994. The Model Communities Programme was a four-year partnership with 14 municipalities that aided with the implementation of LA21. The *Local Agenda 21 Planning Guide* resulting from the project continues to be used by municipalities worldwide, and has been translated into numerous languages.

The Canadian Sustainable Cities Initiative promotes targeted multi-sectoral partnerships involving municipalities, small and large companies, NGOs and community-based organizations and governments. It uses integrated approaches to address issues such as urban transportation, waste management, clean energy, and urban planning – all in support of sustainable economic development and improving quality of life without compromising the future. Five projects have been initiated – in Salvador, Brazil; Katowice, Poland; Qingdao, China; Cordoba, Argentina; and San Jose, Costa Rica. These projects provide a useful example of leveraged partnerships – between Canada and other countries, and among Canadian organizations – in support of sustainable development.

4.4 Continuing Challenges

Canada is one of the most highly urbanized countries in the world. Its economic prosperity depends to a large degree on the efficient functioning of its cities. A recent trend in intergovernmental relations in Canada is the transfer down to local and regional governments of provincial authority in areas such as social services, often without the required human and financial resources to carry out the new responsibilities.

Confronted by 21st century urban problems, cities remain governed by a model that was designed in the 19th century, a time when large cities were practically non-existent. In Canada, financial support for local governments has increased only minimally over the last 10 years, even as they take on greater responsibility for social and other services. Despite the transfer of new responsibilities from many provinces, municipal authority to raise revenues through local taxation remains significantly constrained (Montreal and the Greater Vancouver Regional District are two of the only Canadian cities to receive a portion of provincial gasoline taxes). Without appropriate resources, tools and authority, Canadian cities are finding it increasingly difficult to respond effectively to the sustainability challenges they face.

> *"Because a shift toward more sustainable forms of development requires above all important changes in decision-making, the challenge of creating an appropriate governance framework and the necessary tools to assist local efforts is critical to the success of Canada's efforts to achieve sustainable communities."*
>
> **David Bell and Michelle Grinstein**
> **York University, Centre for Applied Sustainability**

Sustainable Communities

5 HEALTH AND ENVIRONMENT

A recent federal-provincial report on the health of our population, *Towards a Healthy Future: Second Report on the Health of Canadians*, notes that: "We have one of the safest food supplies in the world, the overall quality of our air and drinking water is good, and the built (or human-made) environment is generally clean and healthy." There is growing scientific acceptance that environmental quality is a major determinant of human health – that the health of Canadians is influenced by air they breathe, the water they drink, the food they eat, and the places in which they live. Canadian public opinion is increasingly making the link between health and environmental quality. In a 2000 survey, 89 per cent of Canadians agreed that the effects of pollution are already affecting the health of children, and in a separate survey, 61 per cent reported being "very concerned about air quality."

In addition to these general concerns, Canada has several populations whose health is particularly vulnerable to environmental degradation. As signatory to the Miami Declaration on Children's Environmental Health, Canada has acknowledged that children throughout the world "face significant threats from an array of environmental hazards." Children are particularly vulnerable to pollution and ecotoxicity for a number of reasons:

- In-utero exposure of the developing fetus to persistent organic pollutants (POPs) can disrupt organ differentiation and other important processes.
- Children have proportionately higher exposure than adults because they eat more food, drink more water, and breathe more air per kilogram of bodyweight.
- Their metabolic systems are immature at birth and for some months, even years afterwards, so they do not detoxify and excrete pollutants as well as adults do.
- From conception through to adolescence, children are growing and developing rapidly and their organ systems are differentiating and maturing. These processes are sensitive to disruptions that may have life-long effects.
- Children's behaviour – crawling, breathing at tailpipe level, consuming significant amounts of soil, and exploring their environment – increase their exposure and vulnerability to environmental contaminants.
- Children have many more years of life ahead of them than adults, giving time for long-term effects to be felt.

Canada's Aboriginal population is particularly vulnerable to contaminants in traditional/country foods, and poor indoor air and water quality on Aboriginal reserves. For example, numerous studies have found that levels of certain organo-chlorines and heavy metals such as mercury are significantly higher in the breast milk of Inuit women than among women in southern Canada.

Canadian action on health and environment must therefore be judged not only on the basis of national average health status, but also relative to the needs of these and other vulnerable populations.

5.1 AIR

Air quality is a major concern for large urban centers, particularly those located in the Windsor-to-Quebec corridor, the lower Fraser Valley (in British Columbia) and the southern Atlantic region. In summer, more than half of all Canadians are routinely exposed to ozone levels that are known to have adverse effects on health.

Canada's understanding of the complex interaction between air quality and human and ecosystem health has improved significantly over the past decade. A recent study by the Ontario Medical Association, for example, estimates that current levels of air pollution in Ontario alone are responsible for 1,900 deaths, 9,800 hospital admissions, 13,000 emergency room visits and 47 million minor illness days. The same study estimates that current levels of air pollution in Canada's largest province are responsible for $600 million annually in direct medical costs and about the same amount in direct costs to employers and employees for lost time. Indirect costs related to pain and suffering and the value of premature deaths may be as high as an additional $9 billion. Scientists have also found that the impacts of air pollution on chronic bronchitis and asthma occur at lower levels of exposure than previously thought.

Ground-level ozone/smog presents one of the most difficult air pollution challenges for Canadians. The increased knowledge about the health effects of particulate matter and ground level ozone has refocused management efforts on these issues. Recent initiatives include:
- Canada-wide Standards on particulate matter, ozone, benzene, mercury and dioxin and furans.
- The 1998 Canada-Wide Acid Rain Strategy for Post-2000.
- The 2000 Ozone Annex to the 1991 Canada-US Air Quality Agreement. It is estimated that initiatives implemented to meet commitments under the Annex will result in emission reductions of nitrogen oxides and volatile organic compounds of 39 and 18 per cent of 1990 levels by 2007.
- Ongoing upgrades to the National Air Pollution Surveillance (NAPS) Network and the Canadian Air and Precipitation Monitoring Network (CAPMON) to provide more detailed data on smog-causing air pollutants including particulate matter, ozone, sulphur dioxide, carbon monoxide, nitrogen oxides (NOx) and volatile organic compounds (VOCs).

- Expanded air quality forecasting and real-time reporting programs to provide Canadians with information to modify their activities, protect their health and reduce their contribution to air pollution. Some fifty-six per cent of Canadians now receive daily summertime smog forecasts extending from one to three days.

But not all efforts have been timely. In the late 1980s, for example, numerous cities in Canada experienced record levels of smog. In response, federal and provincial governments developed a NOx/VOC management plan. However, with limited exceptions (such as the Lower Fraser Valley region of British Columbia), implementation was slow, and by the end of 1990s the Federal Auditor General noted the lack of progress in addressing urban smog.

In addition, some positive trends are reversing themselves. While outdoor air pollution in Canada fell from over 120 "fair" days and over 40 "poor" days in 1980 to roughly 50 "fair" and less than 10 "poor" days in 1994, this trend has been reversed since then in some urban centers because of higher levels of ground-level ozone and fine airborne particles. Levels of ground-level ozone and particulates have consistently been close to maximum acceptable levels for the past 20 and 15 years, respectively, in major southern cities. These levels increased in the late 1990s.

> In 1994, the Alberta Cabinet delegated responsibility for air quality management to the *Clean Air Strategic Alliance (CASA)*, a partnership of government, industry and NGOs. CASA input has resulted in:
> - re-design of the provincial ambient air quality monitoring system and creation of an on-line data base;
> - an improved SO_2 management system; and
> - critical, target and monitoring loads for the evaluation and management of acid deposition.

While the co-benefits are clear of improving energy efficiency and promoting renewable energy sources, most provincial and federal government actions have not made a strong link between these issues. The federal government's *Action Plan 2000 on Climate Change* contains a commitment to develop and deploy alternative energy in Canada, reducing both greenhouse gases and smog forming pollutants. *Action Plan 2000* also includes a Motor Vehicle Fuel Efficiency Initiative, targeting a significant voluntary improvement in new vehicle fuel efficiency by 2010, as well as a comprehensive public education campaign to promote 'green' driving.

> The June 11, 2001 Memorandum of Understanding among Environment Canada, the Canadian Vehicle Manufacturers' Association and the Association of International Automobile Manufacturers of Canada, commits vehicle manufacturers to market in Canada the same model year 2001-2003 low-emission passenger cars and light-duty trucks as those sold in the U.S. under the Voluntary National Low-Emission Vehicle Program.

The federal government has also recently provided support for renewable energy production, including an incentive for wind power (up to $260 million over 15 years). Notwithstanding these initiatives, the federal government continues to wrestle with the challenge of integrating energy policies with its various ongoing initiatives to address air pollution from some of Canada's most energy intensive sectors.

Canada has also had partial success in addressing air pollution from vehicles. While individual North American vehicles emit 97 per cent fewer hydrocarbons, 95 per cent less carbon monoxide and 83 per cent fewer nitrogen oxides compared to 1971, and Canada banned lead additives in gasoline for on-road vehicles in 1990, there are many more cars on the road and most jurisdictions have been slow to follow the lead of British Columbia in requiring reduced emissions from the entire vehicle fleet, including vans, light trucks and sport utility vehicles. Recently, the Federal Government announced a 10-year agenda for cleaner vehicles, engines and fuels. This agenda includes new vehicle and engine standards for diesel fuel used in trucks, buses and construction and agricultural equipment by 2004.

Figure 5.1: Number of Days of Fair and Poor Air Quality in Canadian Cities

Health and Environment

Indoor air quality also poses challenges. Indoor air pollutants include a number of substances known to act as initiators or triggers of asthma. Indoor air may also contain high levels of volatile organic compounds, because of the wide range of synthetic materials and products used in buildings. Ironically, some earlier Canadian efforts to improve energy efficiency have had unwanted impacts on indoor air quality. Canadian efforts to improve building energy efficiency, by improving the sealing of buildings, have exacerbated these problems. The "sealed building syndrome" is an ongoing cause of concern.

5.2 WATER

Canada's water quality remains good when compared to most other countries, and Canada is fortunate to have access to large quantities of clean freshwater, although much of this water is in the North, far from major population centres. However, as demonstrated by incidents of water contamination (two examples are in Walkerton, Ontario and North Battleford, Saskatchewan)[2], several Canadian communities face periodic threats to the quality of their water from municipal wastewater effluent, industrial effluent, urban and agricultural runoff, septic systems and various land use practices.

Canadians consume 350 litres of water a day per capita, second only to Americans as the most profligate consumers of water in the world. The average global citizen needs only between 20 and 40 litres of water a day for drinking and sanitation. Our high per capita water usage, coupled with other stressors such as population growth, creates rising pressures on Canada's freshwater resources.

Technology has been a principal focus for addressing biological and chemical contamination in drinking water in Canada. Drinking water treatment and wastewater effluent treatment are now commonplace for most Canadian municipalities, but not in many Aboriginal communities. Although treatment has greatly contributed to the overall safety of the water supply, these systems have limitations and may generate health concerns of their own. Chlorination, one of the principal tools used in Canada for the disinfection of drinking water, generates a host of by-products that either have, or are suspected of having, carcinogenic properties. Health Canada, for example, has suggested that the long-term consumption of chlorinated surface water with elevated levels of trihalomethanes (formed when disinfectants

---

[2] In 2002, the Walkerton Inquiry reported that waterborne disease outbreaks probably occur more often than are reported, at least in Ontario. There were 39 published reports on waterborne outbreaks in Ontario between 1974 and 2000. There were 542 pollution-related boil water advisories in Quebec in 2000. British Columbia issues an average of 250 'boil water' advisories a year, most as a result of water contamination. Newfoundland issued 250 boil water advisories in 2001 as a result of water contamination or chlorine treatment deficiencies.

such as chlorine react with naturally-occurring organic matter in water) may be associated with an increased risk of bladder cancer and possibly colon cancer.

Technology will continue to be an important component of drinking water protection in Canada. Canadian technology enhancements such as ultra-filtration and UV sterilization are offering alternatives to chlorination that may help reduce chlorination by-products that are considered potential carcinogens. Canadian governments are also paying increasing attention to the need for better source water and ground water protection. In some areas, this includes a more strategic approach to managing water quality, involving increased cooperation across the municipal, provincial, territorial and federal governments on such issues as agricultural run-off and better source water protection, as well as recent announcements by a number of provinces about the development of new water resource management strategies.

Remedial Action Plan

In 1985, the Governments of Canada and the United States, in cooperation with the International Joint Commission, identified "Areas of Concern" around the Canada-US Great Lakes (17 in Canada) where industrial, agricultural, and municipal activities were creating stress on the surrounding ecosystems. Native fish, bird, mammal, and plant species were being lost to these stresses and further pressures from contamination of water and sediments; recreational activities such as fishing and swimming were disappearing because of health concerns. The Great Lakes Remedial Action Plan (RAP) program was formalized in the 1987 amendment to the Canada-United States Great Lakes Water Quality Agreement. The program began as a partnership among federal, provincial and local agencies to restore the areas of concern to a more natural state. The mission of the RAPs is to restore beneficial uses in degraded areas within the basin. While the RAP process has been successful in engaging local communities and industries, and in creating partnerships among all levels of government, progress has been slow. Only one Area of Concern has been removed from the list of sites, that of Collingwood Harbour in Ontario.

Over the past ten years, various federal/provincial/territorial mechanisms have developed numerous water quality guidelines. These guidelines are non-binding, but provide quantitative statements on what pollutant levels do not compromise health and the integrity of the environment. Over 80 of them are drinking water quality guidelines. The federal government uses these drinking water guidelines to ensure the safety of drinking water on federal lands and to establish the link between contaminants and waterborne diseases. Provinces use them for setting provincial standards. There are also over 200 Canadian Environmental Quality Guidelines related to ambient water quality for recreational use, maintenance of healthy freshwater and marine aquatic life, sediments, and agricultural practices.

It is likely that additional measures will be required to remedy existing problems and to prevent future risks with respect to drinking water. In particular, serious questions are being posed as to whether national guidelines or more stringent standards and regulations are the most appropriate tools to manage water quality.

One important new development is that the federal government is now reviewing the toxicological characteristics of numerous pharmaceuticals, veterinary drugs, food additives, cosmetics and various consumer products previously not assessed for their potential to harm human health or the environment. Many of these substances are present in municipal wastewater and agricultural run-off. As well, many of the substances found in products newly introduced into Canadian markets will be addressed under the *Canadian Environmental Protection Act, 1999*, or other federal legislation.

As with air quality, Canada shares many water issues with the U.S. In 1909, Canada and the U.S. signed the *Boundary Waters Treaty* to govern shared water resources. An independent International Joint Commission was created to address issues related to the *Treaty*. The *Treaty* is a landmark in Canada-U.S. relations, illustrating the cooperative approach both countries have adopted to managing transboundary questions.

A key priority in protecting human health and environmental quality in Canada is enhanced knowledge regarding groundwater. Groundwater is often the main source of water to sustain ecosystems, riparian zones and lakes and rivers. It is the source of potable water for approximately 30 per cent of Canadians. Over the past decade, the federal government, in partnership with provincial agencies, universities, and the private sector, has completed several new regional projects across Canada. This work is a critical component in protecting the health of Canadians and the environmental quality of Canada's freshwater resources.

Regional ecosystem initiatives represent another important approach. They have helped Canadians achieve environmental results by generating a broad local basis of support for shared priorities for research and action, as well as through public-private partnerships and pooled resources and local capacity enhancement. Large ecosystem initiatives have included: the Atlantic Coastal Action Program; the St. Lawrence Action Plan Vision 2000; Great Lakes 2000; the Northern River Basins Study/Northern Rivers Ecosystem Initiative; and the Fraser River Action Plan/Georgia Basin Ecosystem Initiative. In every case, these initiatives have involved the federal government, the affected provinces and multiple stakeholders at every level.

An Example of an Ecosystem Initiative: The St. Lawrence Action Plan

Now in its third phase, the St. Lawrence Action Plan, first launched in 1988 by the federal and provincial governments, is one of the largest environmental initiatives for the protection and conservation of Canada's major ecosystems.

Reduction of Toxic Substances

Since 1988, 106 industrial plants have decreased their toxic discharges into the River. This reduction has been supported by the implementation and funding of over 130 technological development projects. An environmental monitoring programme and an integrated oceanographic and environmental information system allow for monitoring the state of the river. Improvements have been noted in the quality of sediments and water, and concentrations of chemical contaminants in fish and plants have decreased.

Towards Sustainable Navigation

Shipping and boating is a new component of the Plan. Among the issues to be dealt with are dredging, contaminated site management and sediment management, riverbank protection, ballast waters, commercial shipping and pleasure boating practices.

Maintenance of Biodiversity

The Plan has helped protect 12,700 hectares of wildlife habitat, implemented various wetlands development and restoration pilot projects, and has led to the creation of the Saguenay-St. Lawrence Marine Park, and the implementation of recovery plans for 27 threatened species. The most recent survey of the beluga population in the St. Lawrence indicates that its numbers are stabilizing, although it retains its designation as an endangered species.

Community Involvement

The ZIP (Area of Prime Concern) Program brought together more than 2,000 people to identify local priorities for action, leading to the development of 11 Environmental Remedial Action Plans and various integrated coastal zone management plans.

Agricultural Clean-up

As a result of evidence of the presence of herbicides used on field crops in several tributaries and the St. Lawrence, agricultural clean-up action plans are being undertaken in the drainage basins of several rivers.

Managing in Partnership and Significant Economic Spin-offs

The Plan's collaborative mechanisms involve the private sector, universities, research centres, non-governmental organizations and riverside communities. Government investment in the first ten years amounted to over $300 million with other partners investing over $800 million. Tax revenues totaled $208 million, equaling two-thirds of the government investment.

5.3 Toxic Substances

Canadians use many types of chemical substances every day. Some of these play a vital role in enhancing our quality of life and contributing to our economic well-being. However, when released in sufficient amounts into the environment, some of these substances can also threaten human health and ecosystems.

In the last decade, Canadian governments have developed many new tools and approaches to help manage toxic substances. These include strengthening the *Canadian Environmental Protection Act*, launching the Toxic Substances Research Initiative; creating the National Pollutant Release Inventory; leading regional and global efforts to address Persistent Organic Pollutants; launching specific initiatives to reduce mercury releases into the environment; and improving the management of pests and pesticides.

Canadian Environmental Protection Act, 1999

The federal government's principal framework for protecting Canadians and the environment from harmful substances is the *Canadian Environmental Protection Act, 1999 (CEPA 1999)*. The Act requires that all new chemical, polymer and biotechnology substances undergo environmental and health risk assessments prior to manufacture, importation or sale in Canada. It also authorizes the government to control any new or existing substances judged to pose risks to human health or the environment. *CEPA 1999* also represents an important shift in emphasis away from managing pollution after it has been created, towards pollution prevention.

The last 10 to 20 years have shown reductions of persistent and bioaccumulative toxics as measured in key indicator species. Emissions of some key toxics have also been reduced significantly. Through the Great Lakes Ecosystem Initiative, for example, mercury releases to the Great Lakes have been reduced by 78 per cent since 1988. More recent measurements, however, show slight increases in some of the toxic substances that have been monitored since the late 1970s. While there are numerous theories for the slight rebound, they underscore the need for vigilance and increased research. Internationally, there is also rising concern about the long-term effects of environmental contamination on the human immune, reproductive and endocrine systems.

Like other countries, a lack of information is one of the main challenges facing Canadian efforts to manage the risks from toxic substances. There are an estimated 1,000 new chemicals introduced annually, in addition to the over 20,000 already in industrial, agricultural and commercial use in Canada. Information is incomplete about the chemical characteristics, use and exposure patterns, and risks posed by many of these substances. There is even less information available about the specific risks they pose to vulnerable populations such as children and pregnant women. As the Commissioner of the Environment and Sustainable Development has observed, "based on what is known, and considering what is not yet known, their release and exposure remain a cause for concern." The Commissioner further reported in 1999 that "the federal government's ability to detect and understand the effects of toxic substances on Canadians and our ecosystems is seriously threatened."

> *"New evidence is emerging ...that combinations of neuro-toxic chemicals may cause neurological, immune and endocrine system problems.... Of particular concern is the fact that chemicals are tested individually and not in combination, although there is growing evidence of the importance of the interaction of different chemicals."*
>
> **Dr. Trevor Hancock, Chair**
> **Canadian Physicians for the Environment**

Figure 5.2: Persistent Bioaccumulative and Toxic Chemicals in Double-crested Cormorant Eggs

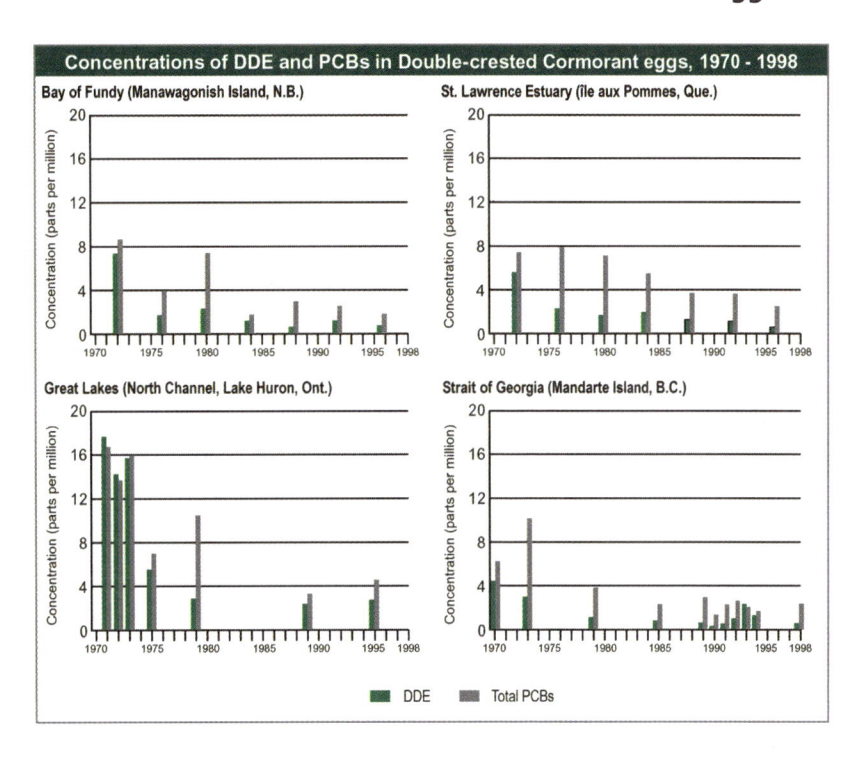

Health and Environment

It is anticipated that the New Substances Notification Regulations under *CEPA, 1999* will help overcome some of the problems with respect to new substances. The regulations effectively reverse the onus of proof onto proponents to provide sufficient evidence to demonstrate the safety of any new substance being introduced into Canada.

Understanding and responding to the legacy of substances already in use in Canada represents a more difficult challenge. *CEPA, 1999* establishes a process similar to the U.S. High Production – High Volume Chemical Challenge and similar processes in Europe. It requires the federal government to characterize, by 2006, the basic toxicological characteristics of the approximately 23,000 substances still available for use today. In some cases, the Act then requires the government to conduct further risk assessments to determine whether a substance poses a risk to human health or the environment.

The 1999 Commissioner of the Environment and Sustainable Development's report on toxics also raised concerns over some of the government's risk management actions, observing that the government has been slow to take action to manage some substances that have been assessed as toxic under CEPA. Some also point to the fact that Canada continues to produce and export substances such as asbestos and some pesticides that are regulated or restricted in Canada. Others argue that Canada's management of toxics does not fully reflect the precautionary principle. Some claim, for example, that reliance on a multi-stakeholder approach results in standards being driven down to the lowest acceptable level among the stakeholders. Critics also argue that the current scientific standard of proof that is required is an unbalanced and unfair burden, given the complexity of the science and the gaps in data and analysis, and as a result there is a high likelihood of undue exposure and possibly irreversible health effects before protective action is taken.

Pesticides represent another important issue that has been the centre of some controversy in Canada. The 1999 Environment Commissioner's report, for example, concluded that the federal government had not yet met its commitments to develop a risk reduction strategy for pesticides. Others point to public pressure for finding alternatives to the use of pesticides in the domestic and agricultural sectors. Among the provinces, Quebec has successfully been reducing the use of agricultural pesticides. A recent decision by the Supreme Court of Canada upheld the authority of a Quebec municipality to ban pesticides from most residential use, thus strengthening the grounds for further local action on this important issue. This decision may lead to further action on local health and environmental issues by municipalities.

5.4 Continuing Challenges

In order to bequeath to future generations the benefits Canada currently enjoys of a safe food supply, overall good air and drinking water quality and a generally clean built (or human-made) environment, Canadian governments will have to continue to make large investments in research, infrastructure, standard-setting and enforcement. Observers and government alike also agree on the need to identify improved indicators of environment-health linkages.

This will require overcoming some of the daunting challenges in understanding the synergistic effects of various toxic substances. More fundamentally, Canada must continue to explore opportunities to prevent pollution through sustainable consumption and production concepts such as life cycle analysis and design for environment. Canada's efforts in these areas have been largely cursory to date. Ultimately, effective action on these issues will require a much closer linkage of industrial and environmental policies than is the case at present.

> *"A central challenge ... is government's ability to address environmental and health issues in an integrated fashion across classical health and environmental jurisdictions and mandates."*
>
> **Bruce Dudley,**
> **The Delphi Group, Ottawa**

Canada will also have to develop effective solutions for a number of emerging concerns, including uncertainty over the balance of benefits and potential environmental and health risks from genetically-modified organisms and the increasing presence of medical drugs in the environment.

The future health of Canadians will also depend on Canada's domestic and international responses to climate change (see chapter 8) and the ongoing decline in biodiversity, both of which could have severe impacts on human health if not addressed appropriately.

6 CONSERVATION AND STEWARDSHIP OF BIODIVERSITY

6.1 BACKGROUND

Canada ratified the Convention on Biological Diversity (CBD) in 1992, and hosts the Convention's permanent Secretariat in Montreal. Since 1992, the federal, provincial, territorial and municipal governments, as well as non-governmental organizations, have collectively made a significant investment in planning how to meet the CBD commitments and other biodiversity-related agreements such as the Convention on International Trade in Endangered Species and the Ramsar Convention on the Protection of Wetlands. A federal Biodiversity Convention Office has guided the development of the Canadian Biodiversity Strategy. The Strategy's five objectives served as the basis for an agreement of federal, provincial and territorial ministers in 2001 on implementing the strategy. The Strategy's goals relate closely with the CBD and are to:

- conserve biodiversity and use biological resources in a sustainable manner;
- improve Canadian understanding of ecosystems and increase resource management capability;
- promote understanding of the need to conserve biological diversity and use biological resources in a sustainable manner;
- maintain or develop incentives and legislation that support the conservation of biodiversity and the sustainable use of biological resources; and
- work with other countries to conserve biodiversity, use biological resources in a sustainable manner, and share equitably the benefits that arise from the utilization of genetic resources.

Some provinces, such as Quebec and Saskatchewan have developed their own biodiversity action plans.

6.2 IDENTIFICATION, MONITORING, AND SYSTEMIZATION

Articles 7a, b, and d of the Convention on Biodiversity commit Parties to identify and monitor the components of biological diversity and to maintain and organize data resulting from these activities. Under the *Accord for the Protection of Species at Risk (1996)*, the federal, provincial and territorial governments are committed to "monitor, assess and report regularly on the status of all wild species" with the objective of identifying those species for which a formal status assessment or additional management attention is necessary. The first collaborative report, *Wild Species 2000: The General Status of Species in Canada*, was released in April 2001, and will be updated every five years.

Canada has more work to do in identifying the total number of species that reside in Canada's terrestrial and marine ecosystems. So far, approximately 71,000 species have been identified, but this number understates the country's true biological wealth, as previously unknown species are still being discovered. While Canada has inventoried most vertebrate species, the knowledge of taxa such as fungi, bacteria, viruses and invertebrates remains rudimentary (a situation also true in other countries).

Canada does not have a reliable baseline against which to measure habitat loss. Analyses that exist show that the highest risk habitats are clustered along the southern border, with hotspots in the prairie regions, southern British Columbia and in a band across eastern Canada stretching from southern Ontario to Nova Scotia. These regions are the most productive agricultural and forestry lands, and contain the highest percentage of species at risk.

With respect to monitoring the status of species, habitats and ecosystems, Environment Canada has taken an important step in establishing the Ecological Monitoring and Assessment Network (EMAN) comprising an informal network of 100 research and monitoring sites across Canada. By encouraging the adoption of standard indicators to monitor various aspects of biodiversity, and by mobilizing a cadre of citizen volunteers through a partnership with an NGO (the Canadian Nature Federation), EMAN is developing an early warning system that detects, describes and reports on changes in Canadian ecosystems at national or ecozone scales. Monitoring the health of species, habitats and ecosystems continues to present challenges.

With respect to information on biodiversity, some jurisdictions (e.g, Ontario) are actively engaged in the development of metadatabases. For its part, the federal government has begun to put in place a Canadian Information System for the Environment to improve the quality and accessibility of all environmental information, including that on biodiversity. However, continuing gaps include the lack of a national catalogue or inventory of existing biological data holdings, the lack of standards for documenting data that would enable information to be used in meta analyses, and insufficient taxonomic expertise to address gaps in species descriptions and identification.

With respect to the development of a national plan and priority system, at the first joint meeting of the federal, provincial and territorial ministers responsible for Wildlife, Forestry, and Fisheries in the fall of 2001, governments agreed to an action plan with inter-jurisdictional priorities for implementing the CBD and to guide research. Building a foundation of biodiversity science and information was identified as a priority, along with monitoring and reporting on biodiversity status and trends. The agreement included a commitment to develop a strategy by the fall of 2002 to enhance the collection, management, sharing, analysis and accessibility of biological information, and to develop a science and research agenda to address the underlying causes of biodiversity loss by the fall of 2003. Ministers also committed to develop a business plan by the fall of 2002 aimed at enhancing the monitoring and integration of biodiversity data across ecosystems, and facilitating regular reporting on biodiversity status and trends in Canada beginning in 2005. A biodiversity stewardship strategy is to be in place by the fall of 2003.

6.3 ENDANGERED SPECIES

Canada is well advanced in accurately identifying threatened and endangered species, especially among vertebrates, birds and fish. The Committee on the Status of Endangered Wildlife in Canada (COSEWIC), composed of federal, provincial, territorial, Aboriginal and non-government representatives, has reviewed and revised the national list of identified species at risk since 1978. Each year it commissions status reports by scientific experts to assess the status of species thought to be at risk. The status of each species is reassessed every 10 years. COSEWIC identified 372 species, subspecies or populations as endangered, threatened or of special concern in 2002.

This number represents a significant increase since Canada ratified the Convention in 1992, attributable in part to an improved ability to identify species at risk. According to *Wild Species 2000: The General Status of Species in Canada*, (April, 2001) 65 per cent of the 1600 species assessed to date are not considered to be endangered, threatened or of special concern; 10 per cent of species are either known to be at risk or may be at risk and there is insufficient data to determine the status of the remaining 25 per cent of species. It is important to note that the priority species were selected for assessment because they are known or suspected to be at risk.

Most species designated to be at risk are in the southern parts of the country, particularly southwest and interior British Columbia, the southern prairies, and southern Ontario. Although the prospects for a number of species have improved, most species considered to be at risk remain in the same state of peril. For some, the situation has become worse.

COSEWIC Status Designations as of May 2002

	Extirpated or Extinct	Endangered	Threatened	Special Concern	Not at Risk	Data Deficient
Mammals	6	18	15	24	46	8
Birds	5	21	8	22	35	2
Amphibians and Reptiles	5	10	16	17	16	2
Fish	7	11	20	36	32	7
Invertebrates	5	11	3	3	1	2
Plants	2	50	37	41	16	4
Mosses	-	2	1	-	-	-
Lichens	-	2	-	4	-	-
TOTAL	30	125	100	147	146	25

Most Canadian jurisdictions have developed the capacity to monitor various species, largely through the creation of provincial conservation data centres (CDCs), that develop tracking lists for species and natural communities, document the occurrence of biodiversity elements, interpret and share data with a wide range of users, and develop scientific methodologies for monitoring and collecting data. The system of CDCs, or their equivalents, now instituted in most provinces, the network of museums across Canada, and new or proposed computer-based archiving and retrieval systems provide the foundation for the establishment of databases for monitoring.

There are many other monitoring initiatives that track the status of various species. Systematic multispecies surveys to monitor abundance of marine fish and invertebrates have been conducted annually since the 1970s on the Atlantic Coast, the Gulf of St. Lawrence, and more recently parts of the Pacific Coast. A program to monitor zooplankton in the Atlantic and Gulf of St. Lawrence was implemented in the 1990s. Volunteer bird monitoring initiatives mobilize citizen scientists to identify and count birds during fall and spring migrations and at other regular times of the year, such as Christmas. Other NGOs fill other gaps in Canada's monitoring network. For example, the Canadian Amphibian and Reptile Conservation Network monitors the status of these species, while the Biological Survey of Canada coordinates scientific research, identification and monitoring of terrestrial arthropods. Through these programs, specialized data sets are being amalgamated into databases throughout Canada.

> **The Peregrine Falcon: An Example of a Successful Recovery**
>
> The Anatum subspecies of the peregrine falcon suffered major population declines in southern Alberta, Manitoba, and the interior of British Columbia and was declared endangered in 1978. It inhabits savanna, agricultural land, seacoast and high mountain, but requires ledges on steep cliffs as nest sites. A pair will establish an exclusive nesting territory that will extend about one kilometre from the nest in any direction and a home range perhaps 50 kilometres across. Thus, this falcon has never been an abundant bird.
>
> Precipitous global declines among falcon populations were associated with the widespread, intensive use of organochloride pesticides such as DDT that cause thinning and breakage of eggshells and reduce hatching success, brood size and breeding. Organochloride contamination has declined substantially since the use of these chemicals was restricted in the 1970s and, increasingly falcons have adapted to using buildings in urban settings as artificial cliffs with ledges suitable for establishing nests. Releases of captive-bred birds have also helped bring about recovery. As of 2000, there are over 500 pairs of Anatum peregrine falcons nesting in Canada. The peregrine falcon was down-listed to Threatened status in 2000.

Although Canada's vast size and limited population have protected it from the extreme landscape alterations that have occurred in other countries, many of the ecosystems in the southern part of the country and in coastal areas are beginning to show the signs of stress that have long been evident in more populous countries. The laws and processes in place to protect biodiversity in Canada are often inadequate in light of the magnitude of the challenge. For example, several of Canada's provinces and territories rely on outdated wildlife laws designed to manage game species for harvest rather than to protect species at risk. The political discretion these laws often allow is particularly controversial.

Federal, provincial and territorial governments have established formal mechanisms for cooperating to prevent species from becoming at risk. In 1996, wildlife ministers from across Canada agreed in principle to the Accord for the Protection of Species at Risk, in which they committed to adopting a common approach to protecting species at risk, including complementary legislation, policies and programs. A new Canadian Endangered Species Conservation Council was established in 1998. The Council is responsible for providing national leadership and direction for preventing wild species from becoming at risk, and has specific responsibilities for overseeing the listing, recovery and monitoring of species that are at risk nationally, as well as for ensuring that good stewardship of natural habitats by all sectors of Canadian society is both recognized and promoted. The long-standing Wildlife Ministers Council of Canada will continue to operate as a forum for federal/provincial/territorial discussion of other wildlife management issues.

Considerable progress has been made in improving the legislative base for the protection of species at risk in Canada since the endorsement of the Accord in 1996. The governments of Nova Scotia and Newfoundland have put legislation in place specifically for the protection of species at risk. For their part, Saskatchewan and Alberta have strengthened existing legislation. Because of the wide range of government tools and voluntary measures to protect species at risk, determining the protection that is actually afforded to species on the ground, however, is difficult.

The federal government has also been proposing to enact legislation to inventory and protect threatened and endangered species since 1996. The proposed federal *Species at Risk Act* (SARA) aims to protect wildlife at risk from becoming extinct or lost from the wild, with the ultimate objective of helping their numbers to recover. SARA is explicitly designed around a cooperative approach that will support voluntary conservation activities and conservation agreements by individuals, organizations, communities, businesses or governments to protect species and habitats.

The proposed Act focuses on species under federal jurisdiction (i.e, on federal lands, aquatic species and species covered by the *Migratory Birds Convention Act)* but includes provisions for federal intervention in other areas where provincial action is deemed insufficient. The proposed SARA builds upon existing laws and agreements and also complements the work done, and to be done, by provincial and territorial governments under the Accord for the Protection of Species at Risk. As well, this new legislation mandates consideration of Aboriginal traditional knowledge as a way to determine both rarity and ecological importance.

Critics of the proposed Act have expressed serious reservations about the federal cabinet (with the advice of a scientific panel) being the final authority for listing threatened species rather than the scientific panel itself. They have also opposed the proposed habitat protection provisions, in particular their reliance on non-regulatory approaches.

6.4 Protected Areas

In response to the recommendations of the World Commission on Environment and Development that each country complete a network of strictly protected areas, Canada undertook in 1992 to "make every effort to complete Canada's networks of protected areas representative of Canada's land-based natural regions by the year 2000 and accelerate the protection of areas representative of Canada's marine natural regions." Although this goal has not yet been met, the results of these efforts have been significant. In total, Canada's parks, environment and wildlife agencies have added over 25 million hectares to the various systems of protected areas since 1992, an area approximately the size of the United Kingdom. Over eight per cent of Canada is now protected according to all IUCN protected area category standards (I through VI).

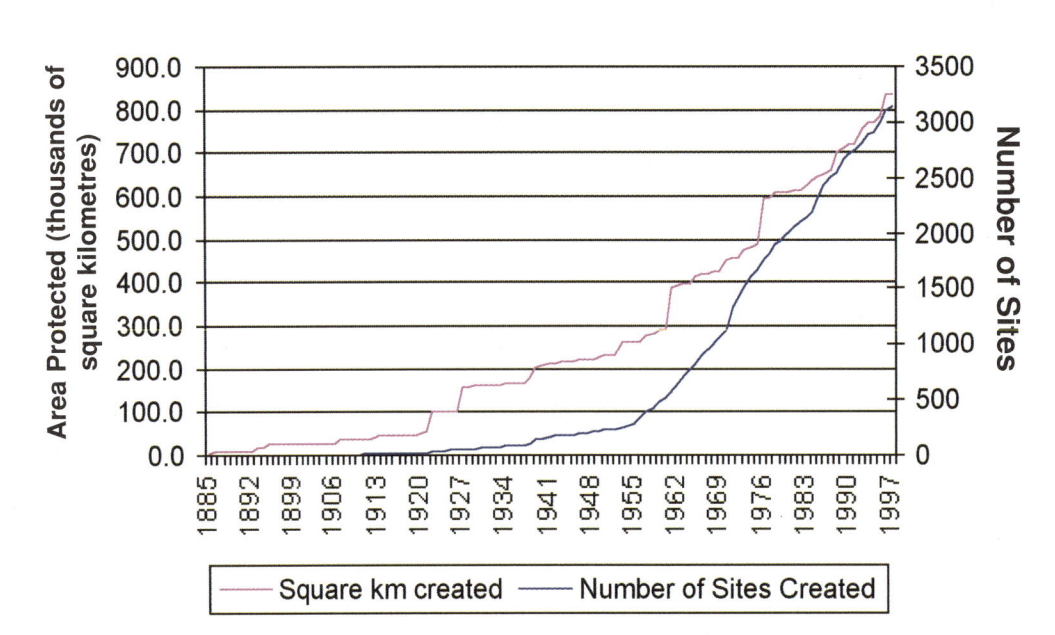

Figure 6.1: Area and Number of Protected Areas in Canada (all IUCN Protected Area Categories)

The Canadian protected area network includes national, provincial and territorial parks and other designations that in total protect over 68 million hectares of nationally and internationally significant habitats. Canada's national park system is roughly two thirds complete, with 14 of its 39 natural regions not yet represented. Lands for national parks within five of these 14 regions have been purchased or reserved from development until negotiations to establish them are complete.

The Endangered Spaces Campaign

Launched by the World Wildlife Fund Canada with the Canadian Parks and Wilderness Society in 1989, the Endangered Spaces campaign mobilized a 10-year effort to complete a national ecologically-representative protected areas network. Collaboration with governments, Aboriginal people, industry, environmental groups and others was fundamental to achieving the campaign objectives. The campaign included the Canadian Wilderness Charter, signed by more than 600,000 Canadians and 300 organizations, making it one of the largest petitions in Canadian history. As a result of these efforts, the federal, provincial and territorial governments established more than 1000 new protected areas, doubling the land protected across Canada. The results showed progress from clear, measurable goals, applied conservation biology and pragmatic negotiation, backed by strong support from the public and government.

Aboriginal people have played an important role in the establishment of new protected areas across the country, particularly in the North. All of the national parks established since 1992 were the result of negotiated agreements between Parks Canada and Aboriginal people, as well as provincial and territorial governments and local communities. The agreements ensure that Aboriginal people maintain their traditional ways of life within these parks, benefit economically from them, and are involved in a cooperative management regime. To date, 11 of Canada's 39 national parks and over 66 per cent of the 244,540 square kilometers of land set aside for national parks and reserves have been achieved with the support of Aboriginal people.

Canadian industry has also contributed to the establishment of new protected areas in recent years by surrendering or donating timber and mineral rights, exploration rights, oil and gas tenures, and land holdings. For example:

- Four companies relinquished their resource rights to an NGO, the Nature Conservancy of Canada, removing a major impediment to the anticipated designation of the Gwaii Haanas National Marine Conservation Area Reserve at some future date.
- Companies voluntarily relinquished development rights, enabling the creation of Grasslands and Vuntut national parks.
- In 1994, West Fraser Timber voluntarily relinquished logging rights to the Kitlope Valley in British Columbia, enabling the creation of the world's largest temperate rainforest protected area.

> ## Ontario's Living Legacy
>
> Ontario's Living Legacy is the most comprehensive natural heritage program in that province's history, establishing 378 new parks and protected areas totaling 2.4 million hectares – the largest single expansion of parks and protected areas ever. The program is a product of the broadest public consultation in Ontario's history, involving industry, environmental groups, anglers, hunters, cottager associations, local municipalities, tourism associations, and individuals.
>
> Living Legacy includes an agreement between the forest industry and the environmental community to work together with government to resolve differences over how public land is used and protected; enhanced protection of fish and wildlife populations, habitats and public access; and strategies to ensure sustainable forestry, mining and tourism industries and increased opportunities for outdoor recreation.

However, as noted, Canada's network of terrestrial and marine protected areas remains incomplete with a significant number of Canadian natural regions inadequately represented in the network, despite the progress made across the country. In recent years, federal and provincial agencies have begun to turn their attention toward the establishment of protected areas in Canada's marine environment. Canada is at a very early stage in its efforts to establish marine protected areas, with a promising start made through emerging legislation and policy. The most recent federal legislation, the proposed *Canada National Marine Conservation Areas Act* (a legislative framework for the establishment and management of national marine conservation areas) was passed by the Senate in June 2002.

> ## Protecting the Marine Environment
>
> In 1995, Canada and over 100 other countries signed the Global Programme of Action for the Protection of the Marine Environment from Land-Based Activities. Canada played a lead role in developing both the Global Programme of Action and a Regional Programme to protect the Arctic. In June 2000, Canada became the first country to launch a National Programme of Action that will be used as a guide for identifying priorities, establishing new actions and strengthening partnerships among governments, Aboriginal people, industry, non-governmental organizations, communities and the Canadian public.

To encourage Canadians to play an active role in protecting environmentally important areas, the federal government established the EcoGifts program in 1995. It provides tax credits for donors of properties certified by the Minister of Environment as ecologically sensitive.

While protected areas have a key role in preserving biodiversity, there is a growing realization that, even when protected, these areas can still come under threat. In March 2000, the Panel on the Ecological Integrity of Canada's National Parks concluded that the national parks were threatened by stresses originating both inside and outside park boundaries: loss and fragmentation of habitat; air pollution; pesticide use; exotic species; and overuse. In response to the report, Parks Canada developed an action plan to make the preservation of ecological integrity the central feature of its operations. A status report and Minister's Round Table have kept stakeholders informed of progress on the action plan.

The *Canada National Parks Act,* proclaimed in 2001, gives Parks Canada a strong legislative framework to deliver on the maintenance and restoration of ecological integrity. The legislation includes provisions for a more expeditious process for the establishment and enlargement of existing national parks, makes the maintenance and restoration of ecological integrity a requirement in all aspects of park management, and strengthens regulation-making authorities.

6.5 Stewardship

In 2000, the Government of Canada introduced a national Habitat Stewardship Program (HSP) in support of protection of habitats used by species at risk. The stewardship program is providing funds to implement conservation actions with non-government organizations and private landowners, conservation groups and local governments, in a broad-based effort to maintain and restore habitat critical to species at risk. This national initiative will see local stewardship projects supported through a $45 million HSP fund over five years.

The job of coordinating recovery efforts for endangered, threatened and extirpated species at risk nationally falls to RENEW (Recovery of Nationally Endangered Wildlife), the national recovery program under the Accord for the Protection of Species at Risk. According to the latest RENEW information, of 118 endangered, 94 threatened and 17 extirpated species on the November 2001 COSEWIC list, 83 species are the direct focus of recovery efforts, while 42 other species are at least partially included in six ecosystem plans and two landscape-scale initiatives benefiting species at risk. There are currently 14 published recovery plans being implemented and 68 other recovery plans or strategies are in draft or under development.

Simultaneously with the creation of RENEW in 1988, Environment Canada and World Wildlife Fund Canada joined forces to establish the Endangered Species Recovery Fund, a partnership that aims at supporting high priority recovery initiatives for species at risk of extinction. This partnership has invested about $6M in on-the-ground projects to date, with an equivalent matching contribution from the recipients.

Sustainable Development: A Canadian Perspective

As part of its national species at risk strategy, the federal government set aside $180 million for the period 2000-01 to 2004-05 for investment in species at risk conservation. In addition, several provinces and territories manage their own rehabilitation programs for species of local interest. Addressing wildlife habitat concerns in a country as large as Canada requires significant financial, human and material resources. Greater efforts will likely be needed in the future to manage wild species.

There are numerous other stewardship projects occurring across Canada aimed at species at risk and at ensuring that common species remain abundant. Legislation in several provinces supports such stewardship projects by providing for conservation easements. To date, some of Canada's most successful stewardship initiatives have been directed at bird species. Efforts to conserve bird habitat began in earnest in the late 1980s, spurred by diminishing waterfowl populations as a result of unabated loss of wetland and upland habitat caused by agricultural and urban expansion. In response to pressure from hunting and conservation communities, Canada and the United States signed the North American Waterfowl Management Plan (NAWMP) in 1986. Mexico joined in 1994. The Plan is a partnership among federal, provincial, state and municipal governments, non-governmental organizations, private companies and individuals. The goal is to return waterfowl populations to their 1970 levels by conserving wetland and upland habitat.

NAWMP partners have committed $1.5 billion over 15 years for habitat enhancement projects. In a very short time, this financial investment produced significant conservation achievements throughout North America. By 2000, 14,000 individual projects had been undertaken with 700,000 hectares of land conserved through acquisition, easements or by changes in land management practices.

A more recent initiative set up under the auspices of the Commission for Environmental Cooperation, the North American Bird Conservation Initiative, is building on the NAWMP model with the objective of maintaining the diversity and abundance of all North American birds through the enhancement of existing initiatives and partnerships.

6.6 CONTINUING CHALLENGES

Although the pace of habitat alteration appears to have slowed in recent decades, biodiversity is still declining and the number of threatened species is growing.

Over the past decade, the rate of ecosystem degradation has continued to outpace efforts at preservation and

> *"The first consideration for Canada must be to invest in its scientific infrastructure which will then guide conservation efforts."*
>
> **Dr. Laura Telford,**
> **Canadian Nature Federation**

restoration, while at the same time demand for precious biological resources is increasing. Canada has a lot of work to do to meet its commitments, but it already has much of the infrastructure and tools in place. The keys to bridging the implementation gap are financial investment; maintenance of the public and political commitment; maintenance of industry commitments; and protection of representative areas before lands are developed or allocated to development.

Programs like NAWMP have shown that large-scale conservation successes are possible over a short time scale where the cooperative mechanisms and financial resources are put in place. In the case of protected areas, the challenge is representing those natural regions that remain un-represented, particularly within the boreal forest and Arctic Canada.

Two emerging challenges will warrant substantial attention in the future: addressing the threat of alien invasive species and engaging stakeholders to act on the third of the CBD's objectives – access to genetic resources and benefit-sharing. The government of Canada has been active in negotiations on the access and benefit-sharing provisions of the CBD over the past two years and will be undertaking further development of a national policy in this area.

7 SUSTAINABLE DEVELOPMENT OF NATURAL RESOURCES

Canadians are stewards of a significant portion of the Earth's resources, both renewable and non-renewable. Natural resource development continues to play a large and increasingly diversified role in the Canadian economy. Over the last decade, Canada has confronted difficult sustainable development issues in a number of natural resource areas: forestry, fisheries, agriculture, and mining and energy. While this section focuses primarily on the forestry and mining sectors, developments in other sectors are also highlighted.

7.1 FORESTS

The forest products industry is a major contributor to Canada's standard of living. It is the largest single contributor to Canada's balance of trade; generates annual sales in excess of $60 billion; directly employs over 370,000 Canadians; is the economic backbone of a large number of communities in a number of provinces including Quebec, Ontario and British Columbia; and is responsible for approximately 2.3 per cent of Canada's GDP.

Over the years, Canada's forests have also been frequent flashpoints of conflict. Environmental, Aboriginal and consumer organizations have all at one time or another expressed concerns about the disappearance of old-growth forests, the destruction of wildlife habitats and the use of specific forestry practices such as clear-cutting.

Canada has been a strong proponent of international action on forests since before the 1992 Rio Conference. At Rio, Canada sought an international convention on forests and helped forge the Statement of Forest Principles. Canada was also instrumental in re-launching the international dialogue on forests after Rio, in cooperation with Malaysia, that helped lay groundwork for the Intergovernmental Panel on Forests (IPF) and the Intergovernmental Forum on Forests (IFF), followed by the UN Forum on Forests established in 2000. Canada continues to promote the development of an international convention on forests.

Management regime

Under the Canadian Constitution, provincial governments are the main stewards of Canada's forests: they manage 71 per cent of Canada's forest land. Provincial governments have each developed their own legislation, regulations, standards and programs through which they allocate forest harvesting rights and management responsibilities. The Government of Ontario, for example, overhauled its legislation in 1994 with the introduction of the *Crown Forest Sustainability Act* (CFSA) and the Policy Framework for Sustainable Forests.

The Framework makes forest sustainability the primary objective of forest management. The CFSA is process-oriented with comprehensive and detailed requirements for the development of forest management plans. One major requirement is the need for extensive consultation with the public and First Nations. Further, the *Ontario Forest Accord* involved representatives of the forest industry, the environmental community and the Ontario government agreeing to a series of commitments to create new parkland, and protect wood supply and jobs in a 39 million hectare area of central and northern Ontario. This provided a mechanism for sharing the forest resource into the future.

As another example, British Columbia brought in a Forest Practices Code that defined the scope and purpose of forest practices, and provided for detailed forest practices to be set out in regulations. The Forest Practices Board was created to audit its implementation. It also created Forest Renewal BC, which spent over $2 billion since 1994 and provided funding and support to communities and workers during the implementation of the Code. In the last few years, the provincial government has undertaken development of a results-based code that will specify acceptable or required results and allow licensees to achieve those results using a variety of approaches.

In 2001, major amendments were made to the *Loi sur les forêts* in Quebec to include several innovative measures to promote sustainable development, including requirements for the maintenance of biodiversity in new forest management plans.

All other provinces have also taken steps to review or revamp their forest policies and legislation over the past decade. Saskatchewan's *Forest Resources Management Act* requires unprecedented levels of public involvement, multilevel planning, independent audits and regular monitoring. Amendments to Nova Scotia's *Forests Act* will enable the government to apply sustainable forest management principles to forest programs on private and public lands throughout the province. Newfoundland was a leader in promoting national indicators for sustainable forest management and has incorporated these indicators into forest ecosystem management plans. Government agencies across Canada have, without exception, adopted a consultative approach to developing forest policy, and routinely seek public views and work closely with industries, Aboriginal groups and environmental organizations to incorporate recreational, social, wildlife and industrial values into forest management planning and decision-making.

Sustainable Development: A Canadian Perspective

> Of the 417.6 million hectares of forests in Canada, 234.5 million hectares are considered "commercial forests," capable of producing commercial species of trees as well as other non-timber benefits. Currently, 119 million hectares of these commercial forests are managed primarily for timber production, while the remaining area has not been accessed or allocated for this purpose. Nineteen per cent of Canada's commercial forest land is classified as being under "policy constraint." This area includes land that will not be harvested due to policy or legislative guidelines: land, for example, that serves as buffers along watercourses or is owned by or managed through agreements with conservation agencies. The non-commercial forest land (183.1 million hectares) is made up of open forests comprising natural areas of small trees, shrubs, and muskegs.
>
> Roughly 0.4 per cent, or about one million hectares, of Canada's commercial forests are harvested yearly. Each province/territory establishes Annual Allowable Cut levels, based on the average volume of wood that may be harvested under sustained yield management. More than half of the area harvested is left to regenerate naturally, usually after some form of preparatory site treatment. The remaining areas are seeded or planted. Roughly 0.5 per cent of Canada's forests are affected by fire, insects, and disease each year and they are also left to regenerate naturally.

Through the Canadian Council of Forest Ministers (CCFM), the 14 federal, provincial and territorial ministers responsible for forests coordinate development of policies and initiatives. The CCFM addresses national and international issues and sets the overall direction for stewardship and sustainable management of Canada's forests. In 1998, the CCFM led the development of Canada's fourth National Forest Strategy (1998-2003) – *Sustainable Forests: A Canadian Commitment*, via a series of cross-country consultations. The 52 governmental and non-governmental organizations that form the National Forest Strategy Coalition have signed the second *Canada Forest Accord* and oversee the Strategy's implementation.

An evaluation of the Strategy to be publicly released in the fall of 2002 will be used as a backdrop to public consultations in the development of a new strategy or accord for 2003-2008. The CCFM has agreed to lead the development of this fifth national forest strategy, in partnership with the members of the National Forest Strategy Coalition. The new strategy or accord will be presented at the 9th National Forest Congress in early 2003, and will be tabled at the XII World Forestry Congress in Quebec City in September 2003.

As a country that accounts for 10 per cent of the world's forest land and almost 20 per cent of global trade in forest products, Canada has played an active role internationally in determining the parameters of sustainable forest management and in implementing the concept on the ground.

In 1993, Canada launched the 'Montreal Process' to help establish criteria and indicators for sustainable forest management in boreal and temperate forests. This process contributed to work on forest indicators internationally, and led to the development of the report *Defining Sustainable Forest Management: A Canadian Approach to Criteria and Indicators*, published by the Canadian Council of Forest Ministers in 1995 (with subsequent reports on indicators in 1997 and 2000). This document has had a far-reaching impact on initiatives to implement sustainable forest management across Canada and was incorporated into the Canadian Standards Association Sustainable Forest Management System standard.

Model Forests

Canada's Model Forest Program, established in 1992, has grown to cover more than six million hectares in 11 sites that represent the major forest regions of Canada. These working model forests bring together industry, environmental groups, community associations, Aboriginal people and governments to develop a common practical approach to sustainable development and forest management. Acting as field laboratories, the forests are being used to test local-level indicators of sustainable forest management.

At Rio, Canada announced its intention to establish an International Model Forest Program based on Canada's domestic model forest program. This has grown to include 19 model forests in 11 countries, in addition to the 11 model forests within Canada. Now renamed the International Model Forest Network Secretariat, it is housed at the International Development Research Centre in Ottawa.

Most provincial governments have adopted the CCFM criteria and indicators as a starting point for assessing sustainable forest management within their jurisdiction. One of the major mechanisms for refining sustainable forest management indicators has come through the Model Forest program (see box).

To encourage sustainable forest management practices by private woodlot owners, in late 2001 the federal government announced a change to the tax treatment of intergenerational transfers of commercial woodlots. This change is aimed at discouraging woodlot owners from prematurely harvesting tree stands in order to generate the revenues required to pay the tax on the intergenerational transfer.

Sustainable forest management has greatly increased the complexity of forest management planning, monitoring and reporting. It has placed a significant burden on forest products companies and on those public interest groups who participate in public consultation processes. Some critics have argued that cuts to government natural resources agency budgets

Sustainable Development of Natural Resources

are reducing the ability of provincial governments, in particular, to keep pace with needed management activities.

The Canadian forest industry has strengthened its forest management and environmental practices in response to market and public pressures as well as government regulation. In the 1990s, it initiated efforts toward the development of sustainable forestry certification standards. Forest certification is a voluntary instrument aimed at promoting sustainable forest management (SFM) through independent, third-party verification that harvesting operations are conducted in a sustainably-managed fashion.

Of the approximately 120 million hectares (ha) of commercially managed forest lands across Canada, as of the end of 2001, approximately nine million ha were certified to Canada's National SFM Standard developed under the Canadian Standards Association; over 8 million ha were certified to the U.S. Sustainable Forest Initiative standard, and 100 thousand ha were certified to the multi-stakeholder managed Forest Stewardship Council principles and criteria for SFM. Industry-wide efforts are underway to have all of their managed forested lands certified under one of the three aforementioned forest specific certification systems.

The environmental record of pulp mills has also improved considerably over the last decade, largely because of a combination of tighter government regulations and market pressures. Since 1989, Canadian pulp and paper mills have invested over $8 billion to increase recycling capacity and to reduce mill emissions and effluents, thereby realizing a:
- 33 per cent reduction in effluent discharge per tonne of product;
- 99 per cent reduction in the generation of chlorinated dioxins and furans;
- 90 per cent reduction in organochlorines in mill effluent;
- 94 per cent reduction in biochemical oxygen demand (BOD);
- 70 per cent reduction in total suspended solids (TSS);
- 9.8 per cent improvement in energy efficiency from 1990 to 1999; and
- 19 per cent reduction in total CO2 emissions even though total production increased by 27 per cent during the same period.

Another important aspect of the Canadian forest products industry's business environment is its link to Aboriginal people. Over the last 10 years there has been a significant increase in the amount of contracts awarded to Aboriginal people for harvesting, road hauling of logs and silviculture. Various forestry companies are helping Aboriginal businesses to develop the expertise and financial capability to capture a larger share of industry work. These efforts have extended to joint ventures with First Nations, such as Iisaak Forest Resources Limited in

British Columbia's Clayoquot Sound, a good example of how Canada has moved from conflict to partnership in managing its forests over the last decade.

In addition, various forest companies are making smaller contracts to allow newer firms a better chance to compete, by lending equipment and developing a database of Aboriginal firms to facilitate contracting. However, Aboriginal people, including the Métis, continue to have limited capacity to participate in, and benefit from, activities in sustainable forest management.

For the past two decades, Canadians have been re-assessing their views of forests and forest practices. In some cases, the debate has evoked deep emotions and resulted in highly polarized confrontations. Nevertheless, over a relatively short period of time, the conflicts regarding forest development and preservation have translated into a widespread dialogue involving communities, governments and a range of local, provincial and national interest groups. The basis for this dialogue is the recognition that forests have multiple values and that solutions can only be found through partnerships that strive to recognize differences in needs and values.

Continuing challenges

Forests are crucial to future generations of Canadians for the environmental, social and economic values they represent. Over the next few years, the Canadian forest products industry will continue to face sustainable development challenges in building on the success to date, including:
- continuing improvement to sustainable forest management practices, including conservation of biodiversity and wildlife habitat;
- embracing market forces as a mechanism for advancing sustainable forest management in this country;
- identifying more precise criteria and indicators to evaluate the industry's social impact in the communities it touches;
- broadening and expanding partnerships with Aboriginal groups and non-governmental organizations to resolve the social and environmental pressures that the industry faces;
- further increasing energy efficiency and reducing greenhouse gases;
- continued adoption of recognized environmental management systems, with third party verification of reporting on processing processes; and
- designing standard mechanisms for measuring and monitoring carbon stocks in forests.

Canadian Commercial Fisheries

Largely as a result of overfishing, the late 1980s and early 1990s witnessed dramatic declines in key stocks of Atlantic groundfish such as Atlantic Cod, accompanied by industry restructuring and major social dislocation in coastal communities. The government's initial response included closing fisheries, retiring licences, and introducing federal income support and assistance programs. Internationally, its response included promoting successful negotiation of the UN Agreement on Straddling Fish Stocks and Highly Migratory Fish Stocks.

In the mid-1990s, some Pacific salmon stocks were also over-exploited, reflecting in part difficulties inherent in managing mixed stock fisheries having a range of users and uses, changing environmental conditions and habitat destruction. The Government responded with measures to rebuild salmon habitat by shifting to selective fishing methods to avoid depressed stocks of salmon stocks, and by retiring licences.

Canadian fisheries have begun to emerge from this difficult period. While the recovery of depressed groundfish stocks has been slow, the Atlantic Canadian fishing industry has regained economic viability through diversification to other species and product development. However, concerns remain over the long-term capacity of commercial fisheries to contribute to the local and national economies as they did in the past. Other oceans-related industries working in tandem with the fishing industry have begun to address issues of ways to more broadly use limited marine resources.

Agriculture

The agriculture and agri-food sector is a $95-billion-a-year industry, exporting more than $21 billion in products each year, and producing almost 10 per cent of Canada's GDP, although its importance varies greatly from one region to another. Canada's agriculture and food industry is a high-tech, high-value, knowledge-based sector. More than 98 per cent of farms are family-owned and operated. A century ago, a Canadian farm grew enough food to feed 12 people annually. Today, with larger farms and productivity that climbs every year, a farm produces enough to feed 135 people every year – and is just as capable of producing fuel ethanol as beef and barley.

Environmental Sustainability

Virtually all the land that is amenable to agricultural production, that is neither built upon nor paved over, is in agricultural use today. The environmental challenges of agricultural production include:

- *Non-point source pollution*: Rural non-point source pollution may come from many possible sources. While the impact of an individual family farm may be very small, cumulatively and if not managed properly, the environmental pressure of agricultural non-point source pollution can damage an ecosystem.

- *Soil erosion*: At a national level, the health of Canada's agricultural soils has generally been maintained or improved over the past 20 years as a result of conservation management practices. However, some soils remain at risk of degradation by erosion, salinization, loss of organic matter, and compaction. This risk is especially high in areas of intensive cultivation.

- *Industrial farming*: Industrial hog farming is the newest addition to the list of environmental concerns in Canada. Factory hog farming produces odours and large amounts of waste that contribute to the pollution of Canadian rivers and adjacent lands, and to global warming. Most of the growth in large-scale hog production is occurring in the Prairie provinces.

Social Sustainability

As economic conditions change, the traditional family farm faces a growing struggle to compete. As a result, Canadian farmers are now relying more on off-farm income and doing a smaller share of their buying and selling locally. Farms are becoming bigger and more mechanized, and require less labour to run.

Economic Sustainability

Farming businesses have been affected by a combination of outside circumstances including increased input costs, historically low market prices, and high levels of foreign subsidies. Commodity prices in certain sectors are extremely low, when compared with inflation and input costs. For example, since 1995 the price of corn has dropped by 46.5 per cent, wheat by 33.9 per cent, and canola by 33.5 per cent. Canadian farm support is substantially lower than that of other countries. For example, in 1997, for every dollar Canadians spent on farm support per capita, Americans spent $2.06, the EU spent $2.14 and Japan spent $3.47.

Grain producers have diversified their production to overcome challenges such as market fluctuations, drought, early frost, trade wars and transportation problems. Because grains and oilseeds are transported long distances in order to reach export markets, producers are largely

> limited to rail. Before August 1, 1995, a national system subsidized transportation charges and guaranteed protection against railway non-performance. However, this system ended in 1995 to comply with the Uruguay Round Agreement on Agriculture on export subsidies and to ease the federal deficit.
>
> Canadian farm support is substantially lower than that of most other OECD countries. However, support in most developing countries, as well as Australia and New Zealand is even lower than Canada's.

7.2 MINING

As one of the world's largest mining nations, Canada produces more than 60 minerals and metals. In 2001, Canada ranked first in the production of potash and uranium, second in nickel, zinc and sulphur, third in aluminum and copper, and fourth in gold. The industry employed almost 395,000 persons, most in high-skilled, high-paying jobs. Mining accounted for 3.4 per cent of GDP and 12.8 per cent of Canadian exports in 2000. The industry has one of the best productivity records of any sector, largely because of ongoing investments in research and high technology. The mining and mineral processing industries spend $325 million on research and development annually and represent five of the top 50 research and development companies in Canada. Canadian mining companies are active in exploration and mining activities around the world.

Canada's federal, provincial and territorial governments play complementary roles in the mining sector. The federal government regulates all uranium mining in Canada, as well as all mining activities on public lands in Yukon, the Northwest Territories and Nunavut. The provincial governments own the natural resources within their jurisdiction, and are responsible for policies and regulations covering exploration, development and extraction of mineral resources as well as the construction, management, reclamation and close-out of mine sites in their jurisdiction. Both levels of government have responsibility for the environmental regulation of the mining industry in their own areas of jurisdiction.

Over the last decade, the Canadian mining industry has been at the centre of intense public debate on key sustainable development issues in Canada and internationally, debate to which the industry began to respond proactively in the 1990s. Some of the issues that have driven this debate include:
- high profile environmental accidents or cases of ongoing serious environmental concerns involving operations, including those owned by Canadian companies in various countries around the world (Guyana, Papua New Guinea and the Philippines); and

- the legacy of abandoned mines across Canada, and the threats to environmental and human health and safety that these raise, according to site-specific circumstances.

Responses by individual companies and collectively by the mining industry have included various efforts to engage stakeholders; development of corporate policies and environmental management systems to support improved environmental, health and safety performance; and development of industry-wide guidelines aimed at addressing specific issues such as the management of tailings facilities.

Mining and sustainable development

Much of the sustainable development agenda for Canadian mining was established in 1992-94 through a comprehensive industry-driven consultation process with stakeholder groups including government, labour unions, Aboriginal peoples, and the environmental community. Dubbed *The Whitehorse Mining Initiative*, it established a set of agreed principles that have since informed the industry's sustainable development initiatives. In 1994, the Mining Association of Canada (MAC) strengthened its environmental policy as a result of this initiative. More recently, in 2000, the Association launched its *Towards Sustainable Mining* initiative to improve the industry's reputation through a demonstrated commitment to sustainable development, improved environmental and social performance, and dialogue with stakeholders. The Initiative is also intended to address broader sustainable development issues such as metals lifecycle responsibility and product stewardship. Internationally, several large Canadian companies are actively participating in the Mining, Minerals and Sustainable Development multi-stakeholder process led by the London-based International Institute for Environment and Development.

> *Toward Sustainable Mining's mandate is "to continue to earn the opportunity to thrive and contribute by demonstrating the social relevance and value of our industry through a stewardship process that aligns our actions with the evolving priorities of our stakeholders."*
>
> *"Reviewing, assessing and assessing industry wide efforts on life cycle analysis and product stewardship is one of the priority issues."*
>
> **Gordon Peeling,**
> **Mining Association of Canada**

Through the 1990s, the mining industry has faced conflicts with biodiversity protection efforts in several provinces and the territories. In most cases issues revolve around competing uses for land that may have high ecological value and at the same time substantial potential for mineral resources. These issues have not been fully resolved in Canada. However, the mining industry has been working with a number of Canadian NGOs, including the Canadian Nature Federation and World Wildlife

Fund Canada, on a range of biodiversity issues. This has included the participation of the Mining Association of Canada (MAC) in a multi-stakeholder partnership to promote new species at risk legislation in Canada. As well, a number of MAC's member companies have made significant investments in land reclamation and other biodiversity-related efforts.

Governments have also been involved in applying the concept of sustainable development to the mining industry. In 1996, the federal government released a policy on the sustainable development of minerals and metals guided by five principles: life-cycle management, risk assessment and risk management, safe use, science and technology, and recycling. Although the policy seeks to reconcile sometimes competing environmental, economic and social imperatives, some environmental groups have criticized it for not placing sufficient emphasis on more efficient production, reduced per capita consumption, increased recycling rates and the avoidance of dissipative uses.

These groups have also raised concerns over the federal government's role in terms of:
- various fiscal measures, such as flow-through shares, that focus on increasing exploration and development activities without addressing sustainability concerns. Such fiscal measures have stimulated increased exploration and development activity, with the attendant environmental and social challenges they raise. Provincial jurisdictions across Canada have incorporated environmental requirements in the permitting of such activities to address these concerns;
- ensuring that activities of the Export Development Corporation (EDC), a public export credit agency, do not support environmentally damaging activities in developing countries. The EDC is now putting in place a revised environmental review framework and principles for corporate social responsibility; and
- the government's position on export of hazardous wastes under the Basel Convention. The Canadian Government, along with many other countries, has not yet taken a final position on ratification of the ban amendment of the Basel Convention restricting export of hazardous wastes from OECD to non-OECD countries. Canada's policy is to support the export of hazardous recyclable materials for use as material inputs to any country that demonstrates that it will be managed in an environmentally sound manner. Canada is currently supporting a Basel Convention study that is researching the possibility of some non-OECD countries receiving some hazardous recyclables if they can demonstrate environmentally sound management. Some Canadian NGOs have criticized the government's position on the Basel Convention ban amendment based on the belief that receiving non-OECD countries could not handle such materials in a manner that is safe for human health and the environment. The Canadian mining industry has been promoting exemption of secondary hazardous materials containing metals from trans-boundary

restrictions under the Basel Convention to facilitate recycling and reduce use of virgin metals.

Sustainable Development of Minerals And Metals

Sustainable development in the context of minerals and metals is considered to incorporate the following elements:

- Finding, extracting, producing, adding value to, using, re-using, recycling, and, when necessary, disposing of mineral and metal products in the most efficient, competitive, and environmentally responsible manner possible, using best practices
- Respecting the needs and values of all resource users and considering those needs and values in government decision-making
- Maintaining or enhancing the quality of life and the environment for present and future generations
- Securing the involvement and participation of stakeholders, individuals, and communities in decision-making.

Natural Resources Canada (1996)
The Minerals and Metals Policy of the Government of Canada:
Partnerships for Sustainable Development

More broadly, Canadian use of metals continues to rise, increasing the environmental stresses associated with mining, production and disposal. The federal government is in the preliminary stages of developing a Resource Recovery Strategy. However, Canada lags behind the US and some European countries in managing metals through their life cycle. At the corporate level, companies in the aluminum, copper, steel and nickel businesses have made substantial investments in metals recovery and recycling, reducing the demand for primary metal sources.

"A weakness in the Canadian approach to sustainability commitments in the metals sector has been a lack of emphasis on reducing consumption, especially of virgin, unrecycled mineral resources."

Alan Young
Environmental Mining Council of British Columbia

Environmental performance

The mining industry has faced a number of environmental performance issues through the 1990s, including acid drainage from tailings and waste rock, metals releases from smelting operations, greenhouse gas releases, and abandoned mines. A recent report determined that there were over 135 acid-generating mines across Canada with an estimated 1.8 billion tonnes of acidic tailings and 700 million tonnes of acid waste rock raising serious concerns for water quality.

The report was produced under the multi-stakeholder Mine Environment Neutral Drainage program, directed at addressing the most serious environmental liability facing the Canadian mining industry. Under the initiative, the mining industry has been developing new technologies and practices for monitoring, treating and preventing acid rock drainage. Nonetheless, significant long-term challenges remain at mine sites across the country to deal with acid mine drainage.

Overall, the Canadian mining industry has significantly reduced its releases of toxic heavy metals over the last decade. It has reduced emissions of:
- arsenic, by 51 per cent;
- cadmium, by 73 per cent;
- lead, by 74 per cent;
- mercury, by 93 per cent; and
- nickel, by 70 per cent.

Nonetheless, releases remain large from metal smelters, with more than 2.3 million pounds of heavy metals reported released in 1998. The five heavy metals reported are declared toxic under the *Canadian Environmental Protection Act, 1999*, with potential serious harmful effects to human health and the environment.

Another area of substantial progress has been the movement towards increased energy efficiency and consequent reductions in greenhouse gas emissions (GHGs). The industry has made substantial improvements in reducing its energy intensity, with significant benefits in cost savings and reduced greenhouse gas emissions. Greenhouse gas emissions in the metal mining sector have been reduced by 24.7 per cent over the period 1990–1999, and GHG intensity as emissions per unit of metal concentrate have been reduced by 13.8 per cent. Coupled with improvements in carbon intensity in metals smelting and refining, the non-ferrous metal sector GHG emissions exceed the Canadian Kyoto commitments.

For their part, both federal and provincial levels of government have tightened the environmental regulation of the mining industry. The federal government, for example, revised the Metal Mining Liquid Effluent Regulations under the *Fisheries Act* and began regulating an increasing number of the toxic emissions in effluent streams. A key feature of these new regulations is environmental effects monitoring. However, NGOs maintain concerns over the completeness of these standards and the lack of government capacity to enforce regulations. The provinces of British Columbia, Saskatchewan, Manitoba, Quebec and Ontario have each launched programs to remediate selected orphaned and abandoned mine sites, and have also tightened regulations governing mine closures. The mining industry has been promoting establishment of a stakeholder advisory committee to address the issue on a national basis. As well, a small number of companies have gone back to reclaim mines they had previously sold.

The experience of the diamond mining industry in the Northwest Territories is an example of Canada's commitment to ensure minimum impact on the environment. To that end, the existing diamond mine and the one currently under construction will be monitored by an independent committee to ensure that impacts during construction, production and closure are minimal and, wherever possible, mitigated on an ongoing basis. The diamond project currently under construction will post one of the largest performance bonds ever required in Canada to ensure that there are adequate funds available to mitigate any existing environmental liabilities during the life of the project.

Social issues

Over the past ten years, the mining industry has made considerable progress in its relationships with Aboriginal people. Through Impact Benefit Agreements, corporate policies and less formal agreements, mining companies have become one of Canada's largest Aboriginal employers. Several companies are investing in Aboriginal training and literacy programs, and have made specific commitments regarding Aboriginal employment.

The importance of Aboriginal-industry partnerships was highlighted in the industry's 2001 submission to federal/provincial/territorial mines ministers that recommended the formation of regional Aboriginal-industry working groups to foster mutual understanding. Notwithstanding this progress, concerns remain over the environmental and social impacts of mining activity affecting Aboriginal people and the need to ensure that negotiations on new mine development address issues of Aboriginal rights.

At the facility level, mining companies have been giving worker health and safety issues more emphasis and several have introduced more effective health and safety management systems. Nonetheless, incidents affecting the health of employees have still occurred. Where there have been incidents, companies have improved their training and monitoring efforts.

More broadly, the Mining Association of Canada's *Toward Sustainable Mining Initiative* has given priority to improving the industry's social responsibility efforts. Some companies have established community advisory groups to help address issues of local development, community health and safety and environmental protection. And while still in early stages of development, other companies have begun to integrate social considerations more directly into project planning and facility operations.

Future challenges

The legacy of abandoned mines – un-reclaimed sites with no known owner – remains a complex challenge in Canada for governments, the mining industry and communities. Other challenges include securing improved local benefits, further increasing metals recovery, recycling and reducing metals use, improving the environmental performance of small operators, and ensuring that appropriate, high standards of environmental, social and ethical performance are consistently applied by Canadian companies operating internationally.

ENERGY IN CANADA

The energy sector is an important part of Canada's economy in terms of investment, trade, income generation, and employment. The energy sector accounts for 6.8 per cent of GDP and 16 per cent of total investment in Canada. However, there are marked regional differences in energy production and consumption.

Fossil fuels are primarily produced from Canada's three western provinces and off its east coast. Significant reserves have also been discovered in Canada's North. Canada is the second-largest producer of hydro-electric power in the world, with Newfoundland and Labrador, Quebec, Ontario, Manitoba and British Columbia accounting for the bulk of Canadian generating capacity. The nuclear power industry, fuelled by domestic uranium, operates 22 CANDU reactors in Canada (mostly in Ontario) and exports its technology around the world. Coal, mined domestically, is the primary fuel for electricity generation in Alberta and Saskatchewan.

Canada has been a net exporter of most energy forms since 1969. The United States is by far Canada's largest customer (91 per cent of Canada's energy exports) and is expected to continue to import large quantities of Canadian energy under the increasingly deregulated market regimes evolving in both countries. The importance of energy in Canada's trade balance is further emphasized when one considers exports of energy-intensive goods, equipment, systems, and expertise.

The production and consumption of energy affects the environment in many significant ways. The production, distribution and consumption of fossil fuels releases carbon dioxide and other air pollutants contributing to urban smog and acid rain. The production of oil from Alberta's oil sands, which account for a rapidly rising share of Canadian production, involves large open-pit mining operations and the need for land reclamation. The damming of large rivers for hydro-electric power (Canada has diverted more rivers for hydro-electric production than any other country in the world) results in large-scale flooding, the destruction of wildlife habitat and, in some cases, has resulted in mercury contamination. Wastes from nuclear energy production raise long-term disposal issues yet to be resolved.

Over the last decade, the federal government has stopped subsidizing energy "megaprojects." It still provides tax incentives to select renewable and efficiency energy technologies and financial support to the nuclear industry ($156 million to the nuclear industry in 2000 and $12 million to renewable energy technologies). Canada's electrical utilities are almost all owned by the provinces in which they are located. In recent years, some provinces have taken steps to privatize their utilities and open electricity generation and distribution to competition.

Low Canadian energy prices have discouraged investments in energy efficiency and explain, in part, Canada's high energy intensity. All levels of government have implemented a variety of programs to promote energy efficiency, alternative transportation fuels and renewable energy.

8 CLIMATE CHANGE

Along with more than 150 countries, Canada signed the United Nations Framework Convention on Climate Change (UNFCCC) at Rio de Janeiro in 1992 and agreed to aim to reduce emissions to 1990 levels by year 2000. Under the Convention, Canada made commitments related to mitigation measures, the preparation of greenhouse gas inventories, the promotion of biological carbon sinks, the transfer of technologies to developing countries, international cooperation in scientific data collection and research, and public education and awareness.

Although Canada contributes only two per cent of global greenhouse gases (GHG) emissions (and the percentage is expected to decrease in the decades to come), Canada is a large per capita emitter. On average, each Canadian emits about 22.5 tonnes of carbon dioxide per year, one of the highest emission rates in the world. Like many other countries, Canada's emissions will be above its stabilization goal in 2000, with emissions increasing by about 15 per cent between 1990 and 1999. Increases in emissions from energy production and distribution, and the transportation sector, have been the main reasons for Canada's inability to stabilize its emissions.

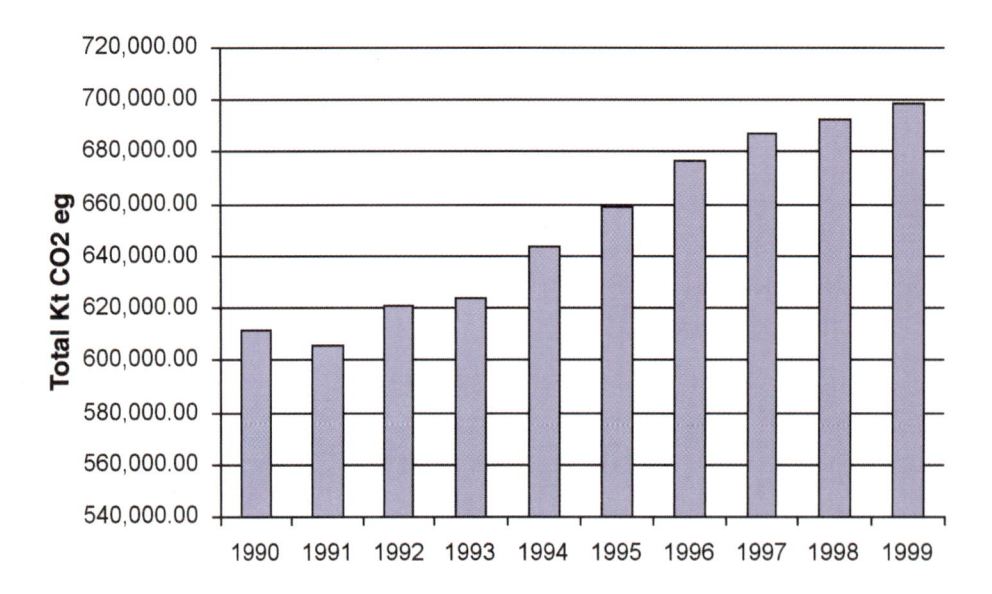

Figure 8.1: Greenhouse Gas Emissions

Canada actively participated in the UNFCCC CoP3 in Japan and signed the Kyoto Protocol in 1997. In the Protocol, Canada agreed to reduce its net GHG emissions by 6 per cent from 1990 levels by the period 2008-2012. Canada expects to take a decision on ratification of the Protocol in 2002.

In 1995, GHG emissions grew by 2.6 per cent while the Canadian economy grew by nearly 3.0 per cent. In comparison, in 1999, GHG emissions grew by just 1.4 per cent while the economy grew by 4.5 per cent. This indicates that the Canadian economy may be growing in a more GHG-efficient manner (and, as seen in chapter 7, some industry sectors have achieved substantial reductions in GHG emissions). In other words, the growth in GHG emissions has slowed while the economy has continued to grow, indicating a possible decoupling between GHG emissions and economic growth. However, in order to achieve the Kyoto target, Canada will have to reduce further the GHG intensity of its economy.

8.1 MITIGATION

Canada's cold climate, the vast distances separating population centres and its economic structure make it an energy-intensive country. Other factors contribute to the major challenge that Canada faces in the development of an effective climate mitigation strategy:

- A population growing more rapidly (11 per cent in the decade to 1999) than that of most other industrialized countries.
- The division of responsibilities between the federal government, and provincial and territorial governments. Provincial governments have responsibility for the management of natural resources, including energy. Some Canadian provinces are significant fossil fuel energy producers, while others are primarily consumers, although almost all produce most of the electrical energy used within their own borders.
- Increased fossil fuel production including that from oil sands and off-shore sources to meet domestic and U.S. demands. Canada exports one-quarter of oil and half of its gas production to the United States. Some of the exported natural gas is used to replace more carbon intensive fossil fuels and thus has the net effect of reducing North America's emissions, even as production-related emissions in Canada increase.
- A low-density urban design, reflecting the expansion of suburbs, particularly since the Second World War. While suburban growth reflects both rising personal incomes and desired lifestyles, it also contributed to urban sprawl. Canada's urban design now accounts for a significant proportion of GHG emissions from the transportation sector.

While Canada has not reached a domestic consensus on a desirable mitigation response to climate change, it has put in place a national process involving all governments and stakeholders to determine an appropriate approach. Some of the key concerns in developing this approach are:

- The concerns by Canadian industry about being placed at a competitive disadvantage with U.S. counterparts and against firms in developing countries that do not have reduction commitments under the Kyoto Protocol. Canadian industry is also concerned about the potential impact on Canada's ability to attract investment relative to its NAFTA partners if Canada ratifies the Protocol and the U.S. does not (Mexico is not obligated to reduce its emissions under the Protocol).
- The concern of several provincial governments about how to balance the anticipated macroeconomic costs of reducing GHG emissions with the uncertain effects of climate change.
- The stronger action advocated by some individual Canadians to reduce emissions, though most have been unwilling to make personal lifestyle changes and the majority remains largely uninformed about the stakes in the debate. In this respect, it should be noted that a more sustained and focused effort to use education as a means of changing public attitudes is required. This will have to involve enhancing the public's understanding of the environmental, societal and economic threats of climate change and motivating individuals toward more effective energy conservation.

Canada's mitigation strategy has relied on a mix of instruments, with a heavy reliance on voluntary measures, and the creation of extensive consultation processes with all the major stakeholders. Internationally, Canada has argued in favour of the various "Kyoto mechanisms" to allow emissions trades and the recognition of biological and soil sequestration of carbon to offset emissions through forestry and agricultural practices. Domestically, governments have also introduced various regulatory and economic measures to reduce GHG emissions, but these have tended to be targeted narrowly.

Canada has also invested significant efforts in identifying, analyzing and consulting on mitigation options. The most ambitious of the consultative arrangements was the formation in 1998 of 16 "Issues Tables" (or committees), drawing upon federal, provincial and municipal agency officials, the relevant industrial sectors, the academic community and non-governmental organizations. The National Climate Change Secretariat coordinated the results of these complex consultations and analyses.

With the help of this Secretariat, the Environment and Energy Ministers of all jurisdictions have agreed to a National Implementation Strategy on Climate Change. In April 1998, Environment and Energy ministers established the National Climate Change Process (NCCP). The NCCP has the mandate to consult stakeholders, evaluate mitigation and adaptation options, and produce national climate change strategies. In October 2000, a major milestone was achieved in the First National Business Plan. The recently released National Climate Change Business Plan 2002 demonstrates the continued efforts of Canada's federal, provincial and territorial governments to manage the risks of climate change by taking individual and joint actions to reduce emissions, to prepare to adapt to a changing environment, and to encourage and enable action by all Canadians. Building upon the primarily governmental focus in the First National Business Plan, the *National Climate Change Business Plan 2002* reflects the truly national effort underway by also profiling some of the many climate change-related activities planned and ongoing by the private sector, municipalities and other public organizations not covered by the First National Business Plan.

In 2000, the federal government announced *Action Plan 2000 on Climate Change* as its contribution to the *First National Climate Change Business Plan*. The government expects that this five-year, $500 million initiative will reduce Canada's greenhouse gas emissions by 65 megatonnes per year by the period 2008-2012 when fully implemented, taking Canada well on the way to its Kyoto target.

Action Plan 2000 contains initiatives in the following areas: transportation, energy (oil and gas production and electricity), industry, buildings, forestry and agriculture, international projects and investing in future solutions (technology, as well as science and adaptation). Federal and provincial/territorial levels of government recognize the opportunity to lead by example and are looking at various ways to reduce the amount of GHG emissions produced from their own operations.

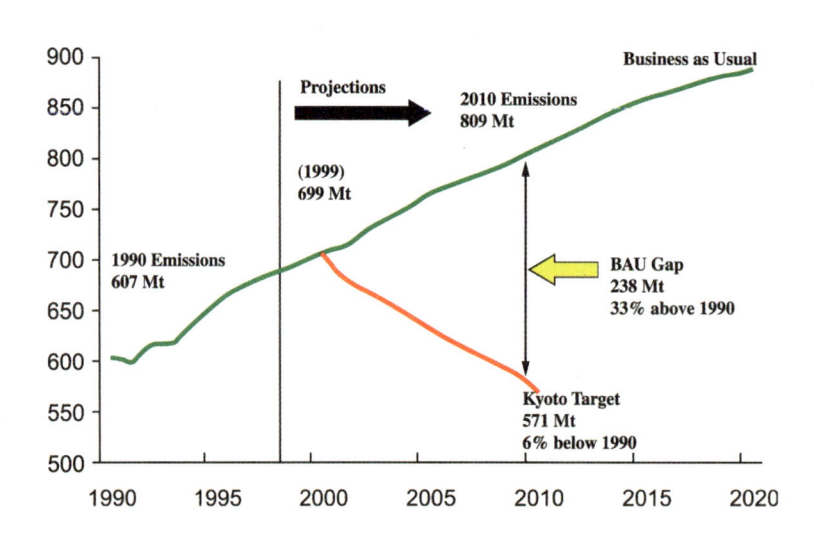

Figure 8.2: Taking Action to Reduce Greenhouse Gas Emissions

- 1990 Emissions 607 Mt
- (1999) 699 Mt
- Projections
- 2010 Emissions 809 Mt
- Business as Usual
- BAU Gap 238 Mt 33% above 1990
- Kyoto Target 571 Mt 6% below 1990

In addition to federal program expenditures to address climate change at the municipal level (see chapter 4), the government has proposed a new production incentive for electricity produced from qualifying wind energy projects. Designed to increase investment in wind energy projects across Canada, the cost of this 15-year program is up to $260 million. As a result of these and other measures, the federal government has committed over $1 billion to climate change programs in the next few years.

As mentioned previously, provincial and territorial governments have a key role to play in a national climate change strategy. In recent years, provincial and territorial governments have put in place their own programs to reduce GHG emissions. These include a mix of public education programs, research, energy efficiency initiatives (such as Saskatchewan's incentives for the residential sector), technology innovation (such as the promotion of wind power in Alberta, Saskatchewan, Ontario, Quebec and Prince Edward Island), demonstration programs (building retrofit and fleet management in several provinces and territories) and regulation. These measures, however, have not prevented GHG emissions from growing in almost every province and territory during the course of the last decade, albeit more slowly than they would have had otherwise.

For most of the 1990s, the Voluntary Challenge Registry (VCR, and EcoGESte in Quebec) was the flagship national program to address climate change. VCR Inc. is a nonprofit partnership between industry and governments that registers participants, records and publishes action plans on its Internet web site, and monitors the progress of voluntary reductions by companies and organizations. As of November 2001, 779 companies and organizations had registered Action Plans, and 368 had submitted Progress Reports. While these action plans describe a long list of measures to reduce GHG emissions, an independent analysis of the voluntary measures taken to date indicates that "emissions of companies making detailed submissions to the VCR do not appear to be rising more slowly than national trends[3]."

Several promising specific initiatives have been taken at the municipal level, supported by federal funding. For example, 33 landfills are recovering about 300 kilotonnes of methane gas each year – enough to heat 150,000 homes. Many building retrofit projects have been undertaken across the country. All save on fuel costs and reduce emissions. Toronto area schools, for example, are now saving $3.8 million per year with retrofit programs that will pay back initial costs in seven to 10 years. Some provinces, including Quebec, have invested in urban public transit to reduce private automobile use.

The Canadian Industry Program For Energy Conservation

For more than 25 years, the Canadian Industry Program for Energy Conservation (CIPEC) has been helping Canadian industry boost its bottom line by using energy more efficiently. CIPEC is a partnership between industry and government that offers a number of services to help each of Canada's industrial sectors develop energy efficiency goals and action plans. Through its 23 task forces that represent more than 4000 companies in all of Canada's industrial sectors, accounting for 95 per cent of secondary industrial energy demand, CIPEC has made it possible to achieve an average annual energy-intensity improvement of 1.3 per cent per year between 1990 and 1998 in spite of greater economic activity. These improvements have helped to reduce the energy-related GHG emissions of CIPEC members below their 1990 levels.

8.2 RESEARCH AND STUDIES

The federal government has made a commitment to science and adaptation studies related to climate change, and Canadian scientific contributions to furthering understanding of climate change have been substantial. Canada has been a major participant in the Intergovernmental Panel on Climate Change (IPCC) scientific assessments that have provided the basis for policy development. A Canadian co-chaired, and Canada provided the secretariat for, Working Group III on Economic and Social Dimensions for the Second Assessment Report. Many Canadian scientists were authors for, and reviewers of, IPCC reports. Through partnerships with universities and the Canadian Climate Research Network, Canada made major advances in climate modelling that led to its extensive international use and recognition of results.

---

[3] Pembina Institute for Appropriate Technology, 2000

Canadian scientists were major participants in projects such as the World Ocean Circulation Experiment, the Global Energy and Water Cycle Experiment, and others of the international global change science agenda.

The federal government's Climate Change Action Fund, started in 1998, injected new funding into climate research, on the natural sciences of the climate system, the impacts of climate change and strategies for adaptation. In 2000, the Canadian government announced the allocation of $60M Canadian to the newly created Canadian Foundation for Climate and Atmospheric Sciences (CFCAS). The CFCAS's mandate is to support academic science in climate variability and climate, air quality, severe weather and marine environmental prediction. The Foundation has already committed about one-half of its resources to research projects in these areas, greatly increasing the support and level of activity in academic research. One continuing concern is the adequacy of support for the government research laboratories, observation networks and related operational services, such as weather and climate forecasting.

> Health Canada has identified eight significant climate change-induced health effects:
> - temperature related morbidity and mortality
> - health effects of extreme weather events
> - air pollution related health effects
> - water and food borne contamination
> - vector borne infectious diseases
> - increased exposure to UV radiation
> - vulnerable populations
> - socio-economic impacts of the above

8.3 ADAPTATION

Climate is one of Canada's defining characteristics. Over long periods of time, natural ecosystems, including the forests that are a major contributor to the Canadian economy, have evolved and adjusted to its climate. Economic and social activities are built around the present climate.

Sustainable development becomes more complex and a more formidable challenge when it must occur against the backdrop of a changing climate. And, in Canada, the climate is changing. The decade of the 1990s is the warmest on record with eight of the last 10 years being warmer than the 1950-80 average (Figure 8.3). In 2001, almost all of Canada was warmer than normal. If the climate were warming slowly, people and ecosystems could perhaps adjust, but the changes observed to date have been dramatic and presage even more significant change. The impact of these changes has been particularly evident in the Canadian Arctic where Inuit have observed changes in ice conditions that hamper their hunting activities.

Figure 8.3: Consecutive Seasons, National Temperature Departures

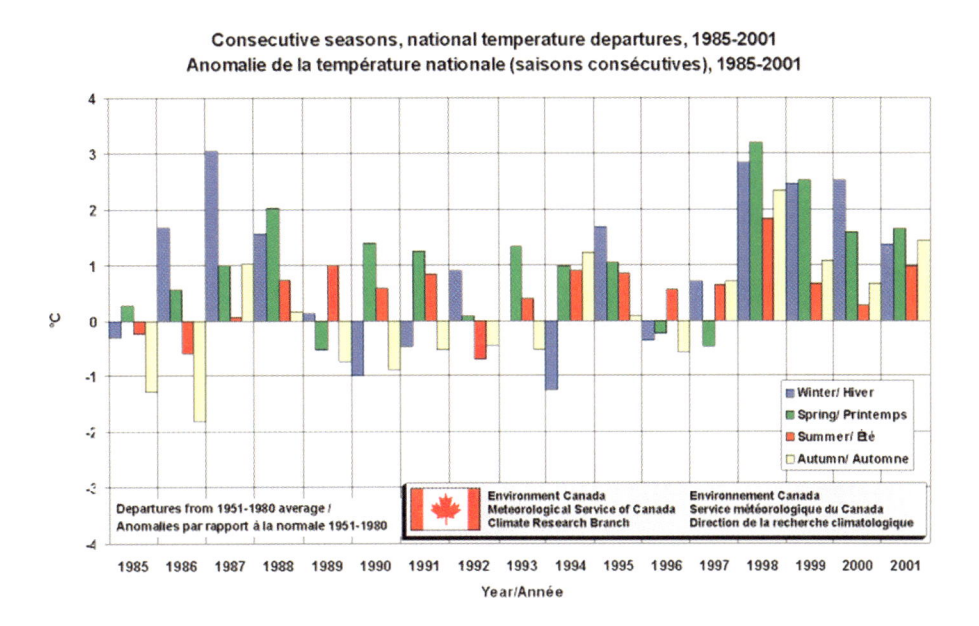

While scientists may not yet have firmly established the link between climate change and individual weather events, Canadians have noticed that the decade of the 1990s was also one of major weather-related events. The Eastern Canada ice storm of 1998 was by far the largest such event in terms of economic cost. It is estimated that Canadians paid more than C$12.5 billion over the decade as a result of major weather-related events such as floods, hailstorms, freezing rain and tornados.

Full implementation of the Kyoto Protocol, while contributing to reducing the rate of warming, will not stabilize the climate. Stabilization of atmospheric carbon dioxide concentrations at any level will require substantial global mitigation of greenhouse gases. Hence, Canada faces challenges in terms of adaptation. While adaptation is possible for most built infrastructure – albeit at a price – for many natural systems, such as the boreal forest, adaptation may be virtually impossible.

Climate Change

Adaptation actions already implemented in Canada include consideration of climate change in the design of the bridge between Prince Edward Island and New Brunswick to allow for sea level rise and changes in ice conditions. Similarly, a number of engineering measures have been adopted in the Mackenzie River basin in the areas where ice-rich permafrost has begun to melt. Anticipating the need for adaptation in food production, Agriculture and Agri-Food Canada is accelerating research on more drought resistant crops. Heat wave/smog alerts have been instituted in Toronto to trigger programs designed to reduce health problems among vulnerable segments of the population. Water conservation measures, additional reservoirs and revised management plans, especially for boundary and trans-boundary waters, are also expected to be required.

Some Anticipated Impacts Of Climate Change In Canada

Being in the northern part of a continent, changes in Canadian climate have already been observed and changes projected for the future are relatively large. According to the *Canada Country Study* undertaken in 1997-98, and more recent work, the impacts are expected to be mainly negative, although there will be some positive effects in a country with a cold winter.

Water Resources: Both projections and observations indicate that river flows and water levels in much of the North will likely increase. However, water availability in southern Canada is likely to continue to decline in summer and autumn low flow seasons, with implications for water supplies, water allocation, hydro-electric production, shipping, waste assimilation, pollution concentrations and freshwater ecosystems.

Agriculture: Higher temperatures and longer frost free seasons combined with increased carbon dioxide in the atmosphere could increase production and permit more diversified crops – providing water supplies are adequate (and larger seasonal moisture deficits are anticipated in all regions of the country). Particularly in the vast grain growing areas of the Prairies, more frequent and intense droughts are likely to offset the more positive effects.

Northwestern Canada and the Arctic: In this region, major disruptions for indigenous people and ecosystems are already occurring. Arctic sea ice thinning is a concern as the losses in ice cover, especially larger than average losses near shore, have made hunting of seals and fish by polar bears and by native communities more dangerous and less productive. Canada is a major contributor to the Arctic Council's Arctic Climate Impact Assessment, examining both bio-physical and socio-economic impacts and will report in 2004.

In Northwestern Canada, soil temperatures have increased by 2 to 4°C, with melting in many areas of ice-rich permafrost. Where this occurs, lands subside, causing failure of building foundations and disruption of roads, watercourses and pipelines. Ice roads, a major means of delivery of supplies to communities in the lower Mackenzie Basin, are now available only later in winter and collapse earlier in spring, increasing food and other supply costs.

Southern Cities: Air pollution and smog episodes in heat waves threaten to be longer and more intense, with increasing sickness and mortality among the young, asthmatics and the elderly.

Sea Level Rise: Rising sea levels, as a result of melting polar ice, will have a devastating effect on coastal wetlands and lowlands, and will threaten coastal infrastructure such as wharves, bridges, causeways, roads, sewage treatment plants and other low-lying structures. A large part of downtown Charlottetown (the capital of Prince Edward Island) would be threatened with flooding from a modest rise in sea level. Such impacts will be accompanied by seawater infiltration of freshwater wells in some coastal areas.

8.4 Continuing Challenges

Canada faces a multi-faceted climate challenge in the decades to come. The Canadian climate is changing and more substantial change in the future seems inevitable. There will be more impacts on Canadian ecosystems and economic activity, and adaptation strategies are needed. At the same time, the Kyoto Protocol commitment of reducing greenhouse gas emissions to six per cent below 1990 levels in the period 2008 to 2012 remains a major challenge for Canada, with the gap between the Kyoto target and business as usual (excluding already announced government measures) currently estimated at 26 per cent.

It is expected that, with no further policy initiatives, 60 per cent of the projected growth in emissions from 2000 to 2010 will come from two sectors: transportation (31 per cent) and fossil fuel production (29 per cent). Indeed, it will be difficult to find a way to meet Canada's Kyoto target without significant action to reduce emissions from the transportation sector. This sector, counting both passenger and freight, is now the largest source of GHG emissions and is growing more rapidly than any other.

The challenge for Canada in the transportation sector is to break the historical link between economic growth and increased transportation activity leading to higher GHG emissions. Making this break will require a balance of technology, behaviour change and infrastructure investment that takes into account the integrated nature of the North American transportation system.

Hence, Canada must look for the combination of instruments, policies and approaches that address its international commitments (including the Kyoto emission reduction target), finds the optimum adaptation strategies for Canada, and maximizes the co-benefits of its climate, air pollution, biodiversity and other related strategies.

9 THE CANADIAN ARCTIC

9.1 Background[4]

Until recently, the vast northern regions of Canada were populated solely by indigenous people (Inuit and First Nations). Today, Aboriginal people still make up the majority of residents of the Northwest Territories, Nunavut, Nunavik (in northern Quebec) and northern Labrador. Only in the Yukon has this majority shifted. United by a common language, 41,000 Inuit live in 53 communities in northern Canada, and Aboriginal people make up the majority population in another 46 communities. Non-indigenous people did not take up permanent residence in Canada's Arctic until the early to mid 1900s. Today, increasing numbers of people are making the Arctic their permanent home.

Canada's Arctic is distinctly rural and indigenous in character, and unique in this respect among all of Canada's provinces and territories. More than half the people residing in the Northwest Territories and Nunavut live outside urban areas. Like other Arctic regions, the history of settler migration into Canada's Arctic has been sporadic. In 1898, for example, 30,000 Klondike gold-seekers took up residence in Dawson City, Yukon. By 1910 their population had declined to less than half this number. Boom-bust development, with its negative environmental consequences, remains one of the major challenges facing Canada's Arctic today.

Once viewed as pristine, Canada's Arctic is now known to be suffering from the adverse effects of global environmental phenomena including climate change, the long-range transport of contaminants and ozone depletion. Wind patterns and water currents transport pesticides, PCBs and other persistent organic pollutants (POPs) from industrialized regions in the south, with most sources originating outside Canada. Scientific evidence now supports the circumpolar region's reputation for being a place where these types of pollutants accumulate. Such substances may then biomagnify in the food web, concentrating in the fatty tissue of many Arctic animals, particularly marine mammals, which are, in turn, consumed by Northerners who rely upon "country food."

---

[4] The interested reader may wish to consult three case illustrations commissioned by the Canadian government of the issues discussed in this chapter for the World Summit on Sustainable Development and published separately: (i) Inuit, the Nunavut Land Claims Agreement and the Convention on Biological Diversity; (ii) The Arctic Council as an Example of International Environmental Governance; and (iii) The Arctic, Indigenous Peoples and the Stockholm POPs Convention.

At the global POPs negotiations in Nairobi, Sheila Watt-Cloutier, President of the Inuit Circumpolar Conference (Canada), intervened to help people understand what contaminants in the northern food chain means for Inuit and the world:

"...imagine for a moment if you will the emotions we now feel: shock, panic, grief – as we discover that the food which for generations nourished us and keeps us whole physically and spiritually, is now poisoning us. You go to the supermarket for food. We go out on the land to hunt, fish, trap and gather. The environment is our supermarket. ...As we put our babies to our breasts, we feed them a noxious chemical cocktail that foreshadows neurological disorders, cancers, kidney failure, reproductive dysfunction. That Inuit mothers – far from areas where POPs are manufactured and used – have to think twice before breast-feeding their infants is surely a wake-up call to the world."

Canada recognizes that human health in the Arctic is being compromised by transboundary contaminants – particularly persistent organic pollutants, and is taking action domestically through the Northern Contaminants Program (NCP). The program brings together federal departments, territorial governments and indigenous organizations to develop projects aimed at reducing and, where possible, eliminating contaminants in country food. Key features of the NCP include full partnerships with the northern Aboriginal organizations in the overall management of the program, and the use of traditional knowledge in project implementation and communication strategies.

Internationally, Canada was instrumental in negotiating the *POPs Protocol* to the UN/ECE Convention on Long-range Trans-boundary Air Pollution in 1998 and the global Stockholm *Convention on Persistent Organic Pollutants* in 2001. Canada has ratified both agreements and encourages other nations to do so as well. The *Convention* sets out control measures covering the production, import, export, disposal and use of 12 POPs. While most have been banned or restricted in Canada for years, they are transported from foreign sources through the atmosphere into Canada.

Northern Contaminants Program (NCP)

The NCP was created in 1991 in response to studies showing the presence of contaminants in the Arctic ecosystem. Canada formed a partnership with territorial governments, Aboriginal organizations and university researchers. The aim of the NCP is to work towards reducing and, where possible, eliminating contaminants in traditional/country foods, while providing information that assists informed decision-making by individuals and communities in their food use. Phase 1 (1991–1997) was focused on determining the main sources and pathways of contaminant transport in the Arctic. Phase 2 (1998–2003) is focusing on supporting international controls and clarifying the implications to human health.

There is also mounting evidence that climate change and its associated effects are measurably affecting the Arctic environment, its wildlife and its peoples. As climate and UV models are refined, they support what indigenous peoples are observing – warmer winters, changing ice patterns, shifts in migratory patterns of wildlife, melting permafrost, retreating glaciers and increased burning from exposure to the sun. There is a clear consensus among scientists that temperature changes are expected to be greater in the Arctic than at lower latitudes. Canada and indigenous peoples are building on the successful model used in the global POPs convention negotiations to create a working partnership and introduce an Arctic dimension to strategies for mitigating climate change.

> *"Old Crow residents have noticed that, on Old Crow Flats, lake levels have been dropping over the past 30 years. They are concerned that the Flats are "drying up" from the warmer temperatures and earlier springs of recent years. The waters of the area are becoming clear, devoid of life. Willow shrubs are growing at such a rapid pace that ancestral trails are becoming overgrown and lost. The variety and abundance of bird life is diminishing."*
>
> **Norma Kassi, Vuntut Gwitchin First Nation**
> **Old Crow, Yukon**

The Canadian Arctic

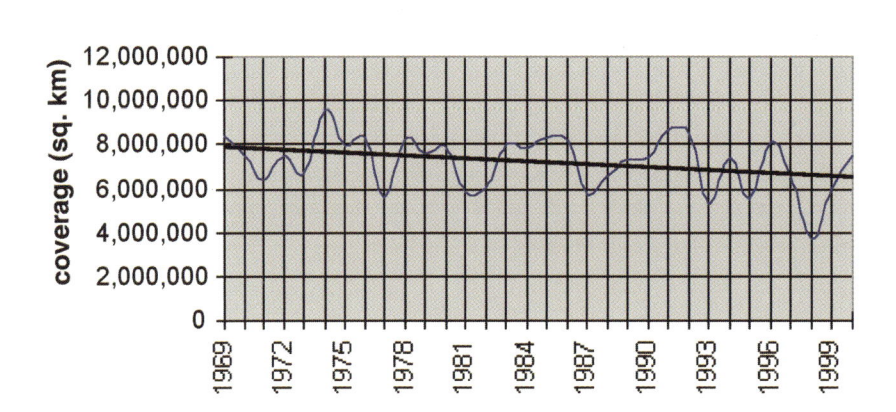

**Figure 9.1: Total Accumulated Ice Coverage
for The Western Canadian Arctic**

The cultural systems and lifestyles of the Arctic, like the ecological systems, are increasingly at risk. Forms of development that may be sustainable in other parts of the world may prove culturally unsustainable in the Arctic. Because cultural integrity is important, not only as an end in itself but also as a condition affecting the sustainable use of natural resources, any strategy designed to promote sustainable development in the Arctic must pay particular attention to helping the region's permanent residents find satisfactory ways to cope with rapid cultural change.

9.2 POLITICAL DEVELOPMENT

In the past 25 years the political landscape of Canada's Arctic has changed dramatically in favour of providing increased opportunities for Northerners to govern themselves according to their particular needs, priorities and visions for the future. The most recent example was the creation of a new and distinct territory in 1999 called Nunavut, in the eastern Arctic, in accord with the wishes of the Inuit majority of the region. Canada is also exploring the transfer of administration and control of a number of responsibilities from the federal to the three territorial governments. Territorial management of land and resources would enhance the territorial governments' range of powers to resemble more closely that enjoyed by the provinces. In the Yukon, the transfer of administration and control over lands and resources is scheduled for implementation in 2003.

Along with the transfer of responsibilities to the territorial governments, the settlement of Aboriginal peoples' land claims in the Arctic is the cornerstone of Canada's commitment to providing a solid foundation for strong local participation in the sustainable and equitable development of lands and resources. The federal government and northern Aboriginal peoples have negotiated comprehensive land claim agreements covering most of Canada's Arctic.

As a result of these agreements, Inuit in northern Canada now own more land than any other non-governmental group or indigenous people in the world, and are equipped with substantial capital funds to assist in economic, political, and cultural development. Very importantly, these agreements also contain co-management regimes where Aboriginal people and government share responsibility for the management of lands, waters and resources. Several of these agreements also contain provisions creating institutions for self-government. By creating new governance institutions and processes, these settlement agreements are designed to promote indigenous cultural and social practices and develop an economic base to support sustainable communities.

YUKON FISH AND WILDLIFE MANAGEMENT BOARD

Established in 1995 under the *Umbrella Final Agreement* with the Council of Yukon Indians, the Yukon Fish and Wildlife Management Board is the primary instrument for the management of fish and wildlife in the Yukon, mandated to make recommendations to the Minister of Renewable Resources on all issues related to fish and wildlife management legislation, research, policies and programs in the Yukon. The Yukon Minister of Renewable Resources appoints the members of the Board, consisting of six recommended by the Council of Yukon First Nations and six by the Government of Yukon.

During the first five years of implementation, the Board has been involved in a wide range of issues including major work on habitat protection, access management, catch and release, and harvest monitoring. It has also been active in recommending new regulations to the Minister for fish and wildlife management in coordination with Renewable Resources Councils, the Yukon Department of Renewable Resources and the public. It has also developed strong ties with Renewable Resources Councils to coordinate input and recommendations concerning local and territory-wide management issues.

9.3 ECONOMIC DEVELOPMENT

Much of the local northern economy can be characterized as a mix of wildlife harvesting, wage employment and social assistance payments. The Arctic region itself, however, continues to offer enormous economic potential for the Canadian economy as a whole from its natural riches of oil, gas and mineral reserves. Consideration is being given to the construction of large-diameter pipelines to bring to market the gas reserves in Canada's North and those in neighbouring Alaska. Recently there have been serious debates surrounding U.S. plans to open the Arctic National Wildlife Refuge in Alaska to hydrocarbon exploration. Canada remains concerned about these proposals because of their potential impacts on the calving grounds of the Porcupine caribou herd, the subject of a 1987 agreement between the governments of Canada and the U.S.

It is mining, however, that remains the economic backbone of all three territories, accounting for the bulk of the gross territorial product, although fluctuations in international mineral prices often lead to pronounced swings in exploration activity and have led to mine closures. Canada's first diamond mine opened recently in the Northwest Territories, with an additional mine to open in 2003 and two more currently in the regulatory process.

In response to these development pressures, northerners and the federal government have established a number of planning and management programs to promote sustainable development. One example is the Beaufort Sea Integrated Management Planning Initiative (BSIMPI), a collaborative effort among government, Aboriginal people (the Inuvialuit) and industry, to ensure that the resources of this sensitive arctic ecosystem are managed in a sustainable manner meeting environmental, economic and socio-cultural needs.

Economic activities – based on renewable resources such as forestry, fishing and tourism – continue to grow and diversify the economy. Aboriginal people face considerable challenges in benefiting from the development of these sectors of the economy: remote access to primary markets, limited transportation infrastructure, lack of capital, lack of post-secondary education and business and commercial skills create an uneven distribution of economic opportunities.

Canada has a strong record for supporting the sustainable use of wildlife resources by Aboriginal people. The European trade ban on wild fur products had a dramatic effect on the local economies of many indigenous communities. Canada and indigenous people took the issue abroad and achieved a Canada-EU Agreement on International Humane Trapping Standards in 1998, an important step in re-establishing the market.

Canada and Aboriginal people have cooperated to protect biodiversity by creating national parks and other protected areas, including marine protected areas, in the Canadian Arctic. Aboriginal people were involved in providing traditional knowledge and expertise in the development of Canada's proposed *Species at Risk Act* legislation. Co-management regimes created under land claims agreements ensure that biodiversity considerations are taken into account in land use planning and resource development.

The Arctic Council

Building on the earlier work of the *Arctic Environmental Protection Strategy*, Canada, Denmark (Greenland), Finland, Iceland, Norway, Russia, Sweden and the United States (Alaska) created the Arctic Council in 1996 as a high-level forum to advance circumpolar cooperation on issues of common concern to Arctic countries and their populations. More specifically, the Council's directives are twofold: to protect the fragile natural environment of the Arctic, and to promote and safeguard the economic, social and cultural well-being of northern peoples. Canada played a key role in the process of developing the Arctic Council, was proud to host its first Secretariat, and was the Council's first chair.

By integrating environmental, economic and social criteria in its considerations and activities, the Council strives for a balanced approach to circumpolar conservation and development issues. Canadian involvement in the Council has helped to form the basis for a successful institutional response to the challenge of sustainable development in the circumpolar region. For example, Canada played a key role in developing a US$30 million project (funded under the World Bank's Global Environmental facility) to implement the *Russian National Program of Action for the Protection of the Arctic Marine Environment* and contributed $1 million to the project.

A unique feature of the Arctic Council is the direct involvement of six indigenous peoples' organizations through their status as 'permanent participants,' assuring that the Council addresses critical matters related to capacity building, and research and education related to sustainable development and environmental protection. This unique arrangement formally recognizes the vital role that indigenous communities of the Arctic have in securing sustainable environmental management and development in the region. Several non-governmental organizations, the Nordic Council of Ministers and the Standing Committee of Arctic Parliamentarians, as well as representatives of non-Arctic states, also participate in the Council as observers.

9.4 Continuing Challenges

Arctic residents, including indigenous peoples, are far better equipped now than in the past to participate forcefully and constructively as partners in national, regional and global political and economic decision-making. Over the past 10 years, many positive changes have occurred in both the policy and legal relationships between Arctic indigenous peoples and government, creating a more equitable basis for the productive partnerships that will continue to emerge. Canada remains committed to sustainable development and working with indigenous peoples and other northerners as they refine their own institutions and craft their own development models.

However, meeting the pressing economic needs of northern communities, especially those of Aboriginal people, while respecting sustainability principles such as environmental protection, human health and respect for cultural diversity, will continue to challenge northerners, governments and industry. Capacity building, improved levels of education, job creation and access to capital are urgent requirements if the benefits from development are to be shared equitably.

10 INTERNATIONAL COOPERATION

At Rio, Canada recognized the need for developed countries to assist developing countries through trade opportunities, debt relief and development cooperation. Specific Canadian commitments included support for a round of global trade negotiations to include the environment, and a reaffirmation of the 0.7 per cent of GDP target for official development assistance (ODA). Canada's national statement at UNCED included a clear reference to the "relationship between poverty and degradation of the environment."

Other Canadian commitments to international environmental cooperation flowing from UNCED include the *Kyoto Protocol*, the *Convention to Combat Desertification*, the *UN Convention on Straddling Fish Stocks*, the *Cartagena Protocol on Biosafety* and the *Convention on Persistent Organic Pollutants*. Although not flowing directly from Rio, Canada has also made commitments to act on the results of a series of social development conferences that broadened the focus of sustainable development internationally. These include the 1995 World Summit for Social Development and its setting of poverty reduction targets, and the Beijing World Conference on Women in 1995, among others. Further, Canada has long been a contributor to the international environmental agenda by advancing and sharing scientific knowledge, as well as through negotiations and policy dialogue in international fora.

On the bilateral front, Canada and the United States have a long history of working together on environmental issues. Canada and the U.S. share a 9,000-kilometre border, 3,900 kilometres of which are formed by boundary waters. The geographic/ecosystem continuity between Canada and the U.S. means that many activities in one country have direct impacts on the health, environment and safety of the other. Currently, there are more than 40 environmental agreements between the federal governments of Canada and the U.S, and over one hundred state and provincial agreements, each supported by solid scientific and operational ties. Canada and the US, along with Mexico, also collaborate on environmental issues through the North American Commission on Environmental Cooperation.

On a regional basis, Canada has been an active participant in the Sound Management of Chemicals working group established under the umbrella of the North American Agreement on Environmental Cooperation. The working group provides a forum for identifying priority pollution issues of concern, developing North American Regional Action Plans to address these priority issues, and overseeing the implementation of approved regional action plans.

International Cooperation

Regional action plans have been agreed on for PCBs, dioxin and furans, DDT, chlordane and mercury. Other ongoing activities cover issues such as hazardous wastes, substance selection for new action plans, and health and children. As described in the preceding chapter, Canada is also actively engaged in the Arctic Council, a unique form of regional governance for sustainable development in the circumpolar north.

10.1 Trade and Sustainable Development

International governance

Over the last decade, Canada has strongly promoted the expansion of free trade internationally and of Canadian trade within free trade agreements. Whether, to what degree, and how environmental and social considerations should be addressed through trade agreements continue to be issues. This is true internationally, where many developing countries have been wary of trade and environment linkages. It is also true domestically, where Canada's trade liberalization efforts occur amid substantial public debate over the economic benefits and environmental and social implications of current and proposed regional and multilateral trade agreements. Public protests over the negotiation of a broader free-trade zone for the Americas in 2001, involving NGOs, labour and faith groups (among others), have raised concerns related to environmental and labour standards and the rights of Aboriginal people.

The federal government has promoted improvements in the governance of the international trade regimes, in part through more effective engagement of developing countries and by promoting transparency in the WTO, as well as strengthening information flow and consultation related to Canadian involvement in trade negotiations.

Canada, together with Mexico and the United States, demonstrated innovation in linking trade and environment through the North American Free Trade Agreement (NAFTA), the first trade agreement to include side agreements on environmental cooperation and labour. Environmental and labour side agreements also have been negotiated to complement trade agreements with Chile and Costa Rica. NAFTA itself has several noteworthy provisions, including preambular articles promoting the strengthening and enforcement of environmental laws and regulations, and a non-binding commitment to not lower environmental standards to attract investment. There is evidence that Mexican environmental law and institutions have been strengthened as a result, although the impact on Canadian and American environmental policies is less clear.

The implementation of NAFTA has raised issues, for example, related to the potential environmental consequences of its Chapter 11 provisions on investment.

Recognizing the link between trade and environment, Canada has undertaken retrospective environmental assessments for the negotiation of NAFTA and of the Uruguay Round, and in February 2001 announced a new *Framework for the Environmental Assessment of International Trade Negotiations* to identify and evaluate environmental effects at the earliest stage of decision-making. Canada has been active in multilateral environmental negotiations and in the WTO's Committee on Trade and Environment. Canada has not yet acceded to the Rotterdam Convention on Prior Informed Consent (PIC) that will regulate trade in banned or severely restricted industrial chemicals and pesticides, although it does follow the PIC procedures that the Convention codifies. Canada is expected to consider ratification of these agreements in 2002, neither of which has yet entered into force.

Market access

Canada has supported improved access to Canadian markets by developing countries. Responding to concerns that access had not improved sufficiently for goods and services in which developing countries have a comparative advantage, Canada expanded its duty-free entry provisions in 2000 to 90 per cent of Canadian tariff lines. Canada also joined in confirming a collective G8 Summit pledge to work toward duty and quota-free access for products originating in least-developed countries. However, like some other OECD countries, Canada has cut less controversial quotas first and has maintained quotas on some of the goods that are of highest value to developing countries.

In the agricultural sector, all raw and processed tropical products (including raw sugar) now enter Canada duty-free, with the exception of refined sugar. As a result of WTO regimes or preferential schemes, essentially all agricultural imports from the least developed and most developing countries enter duty-free to the Canadian market. As a large exporter of agricultural products, Canada has a shared interest with developing countries in substantially reducing trade-distorting domestic agricultural subsidies (see box on agriculture in chapter 7).

Capacity development

Canada has linked its trade and development policies by supporting capacity-building and providing other forms of assistance to developing countries. Since 1991, Canada has provided over $300 million to developing countries in trade-related assistance, of which about $75 million has been for least developed countries. Canada also has supported capacity building and technical assistance programs being coordinated through the new WTO Technical

Cooperation Division, and has advocated the need for trade to be mainstreamed into national development strategies.

For example, the International Development Research Centre (IDRC) has supported developing country researchers to strengthen their capacity in the analysis of trade policies, taking account of issues in the trade-environment debate (such as eco-labelling). Canadian NGOs and policy research groups have also made important contributions. The International Institute for Sustainable Development (IISD), recognized internationally as a non-governmental leader in this field, developed a set of principles for trade and sustainable development that has been used in evolving trade negotiations internationally and regionally. For its part, the North-South Institute has been active in doing forward-looking analysis on Canadian trade policy in the context of the needs of developing countries.

10.2 CANADIAN DEVELOPMENT COOPERATION – FINANCING

Official Development Assistance (ODA) Levels

Canadian ODA levels have dropped since Rio, from 0.49 per cent of GNP in 1991/92 to 0.29 per cent in 1999/2000.

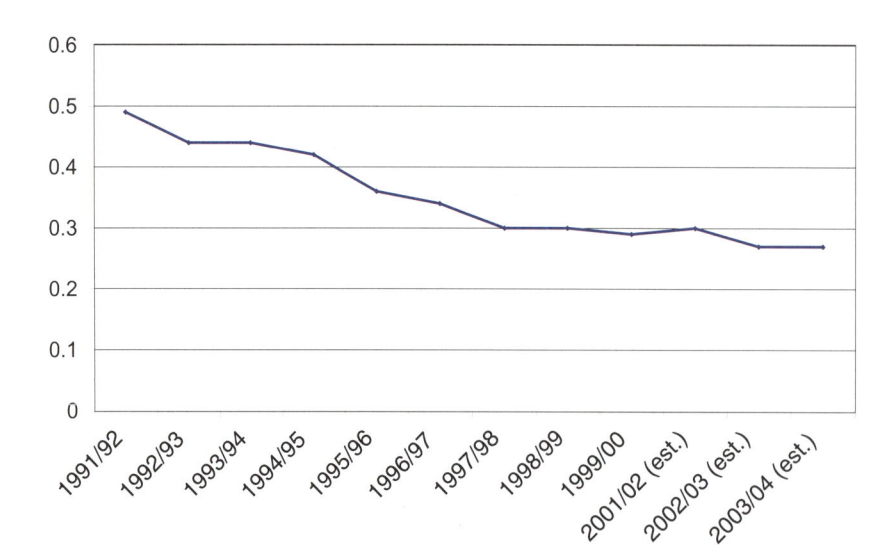

Figure 10.1: Canadian ODA as % GNP

Figure 10.2: International Comparison: Canadian ODA Compared to Other OECD Countries, % GNP, 2000

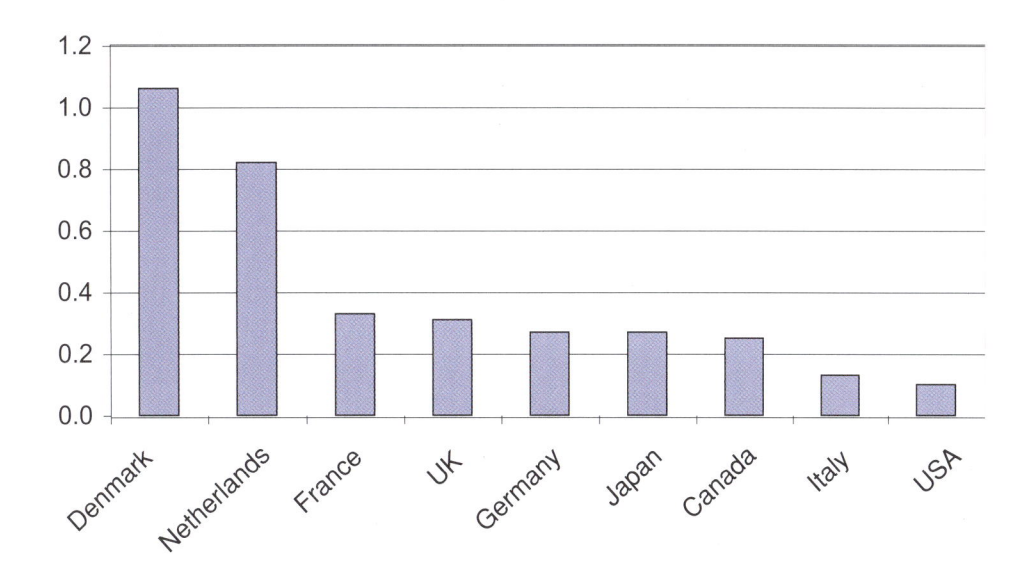

Canada's ODA cuts have included substantial reductions to the budgets of Canadian development education NGOs as well as to bilateral and multilateral programs.

In 2001, the federal government increased its international assistance budget by $1 billion over three years. Among other things, these additional funds will provide

- $500 million to a fund promoting sustainable development in Africa; and
- $100 million in humanitarian and development assistance to Afghanistan.

Civil Society Contributions

Despite, or perhaps in part as a response to this substantial downward trend in ODA, Canadian civil society has responded strongly since Rio, including through financial support for sustainable development. The Canadian Council for International Cooperation (CCIC) has estimated that individual Canadians donated between $350 and $500 million each year for international cooperation work between 1993/94 and 1998/99, although the OECD Development Assistance Committee reports lower figures. A CCIC survey of its members revealed a 25 per cent growth in contributions by individual Canadians over this period, rising to 36 per cent of the total revenues for these not-for-profit development organizations.

International Cooperation

Debt Cancellation and Economic Adjustment

Canada has played a leadership role in debt cancellation for highly indebted countries, both through the efforts of the federal government and Canadian NGOs. Through its efforts in the G20 and G8, it has promoted the cancellation of bilateral debt, including through $125 million of ODA debt swaps for environment in Latin America. In 1999, Canada wrote off 100 per cent of the official commercial debt (EDC and Wheat Board) for the world's six poorest countries. It has also stopped collecting debt service payments from 11 heavily-indebted poor nations that have committed to viable poverty reduction strategies.

Canadian development NGOs and churches have been active in international and domestic efforts to cancel the remaining debt of the poorest countries, working with their counterparts in developing countries to advocate more comprehensive debt solutions. Through the Canadian Jubilee Initiative and the Halifax Initiative there has been activity in highlighting the effects of debt load on the least developed countries, and promoting substantial further progress in the cancellation of bilateral and multilateral official debt. The Initiatives are a Canadian coalition of development, environment, faith, rights and labour groups, and NGOs.

Through its development cooperation efforts, Canada has brought some moderation to international efforts for structural adjustment in developing countries, including promoting reductions in loan conditions, and has supported national governance efforts in developing countries through capacity development for economic management. However, many Canadian NGOs continue to be highly critical of the impact of structural adjustment policies on increasing poverty, and on the environment.

10.3 CANADIAN DEVELOPMENT COOPERATION – FOCUS

Total ODA volume is only one indicator of the depth and seriousness of national commitment to assisting developing countries to promote sustainable development. The focus of this cooperation is another. Since 1995, the Canadian International Development Agency (CIDA) has supported an overarching program goal of "sustainable development in developing countries in order to reduce poverty and to contribute to a more secure, equitable and prosperous world." CIDA has now integrated this commitment to sustainable development into its business planning process. The Canadian development cooperation program has supported a wide range of objectives, countries and domestic interests, a range that many believe has made it difficult for the program to demonstrate clear results necessary to maintain strong public support. There is evidence that multiple objectives relating to broader Canadian foreign policy concerns have at least, in part, deflected support from the poorest countries and peoples.

The CIDA initiative on *Strengthening Aid Effectiveness*, launched in 2001 and involving substantial national consultations, represents an important start to confronting some of the problems caused by its diffuse focus. It is addressing fundamental issues such as geographical concentration, tied aid, and how to improve program effectiveness through responsiveness to local needs and sector concentration.

In this process, Canadian NGOs have called on the government to provide a clear affirmation that poverty eradication is the sole strategic goal for Canadian development cooperation. CIDA's 1995 *Policy on Poverty Reduction* provided a useful framework well before the start of the review. However, while resulting in a number of useful projects, the policy has not been consistently applied in program decision-making.

The International Development Research Centre

As a result of Canada's commitment in Rio, IDRC reoriented its programs explicitly toward sustainable and equitable development, and now supports research in three broad areas – Social and Economic Equity, Environment and Natural Resource Management, and Information and Communication Technologies for Development.

One major focus of IDRC's response to Agenda 21 has been its support of the work of developing country researchers on the management of environment and natural resources, emphasizing the involvement of local communities. These include projects that take an ecosystem approach to human health, an international initiative on environment and health in which IDRC is a world leader, activities on the sustainable use of biodiversity involving research on plant genetic resources and intellectual property rights, international networks on medicinal plant use and conservation, and urban agriculture. The International Model Forest Network, whose Secretariat is based at IDRC, emphasizes the involvement of local communities to build working partnerships at the local level to develop and implement locally-relevant strategies for achieving sustainability in practice.

10.4 Basic Human Needs and Social Development

In 2000, CIDA announced a significant shift in priorities toward four social development priorities to support basic human needs – health and nutrition, basic education, HIV/AIDS and the protection of children, with gender equity an integral component of all four priorities. Distinct from past Canadian development policy statements, this *Framework for Action on Social Development Priorities* has set targets that will see spending increase over five years from a base level of $342 million per year in 1999/2000 to $725 million per year. The result will be a significant rise from a 1999/2000 level of 18 per cent of ODA for these purposes (excluding humanitarian assistance and food aid). IDRC's programme similarly has a major focus on *Social and Economic Equity*, and includes support to researchers in developing countries to develop policies to alleviate poverty and reduce vulnerability, and to improve health delivery systems.

CIDA has been a leader among donor countries in addressing gender dimensions of development throughout the period since Rio, and in 1999 renewed its Policy on Gender Equality to "support women and girls in the realization of their full human rights," consistent with the Beijing Conference *Platform of Action*. Evaluations of the uptake of this and past CIDA gender policies over the last 10 years have shown mixed results, with successful incorporation of gender equality in women-specific projects, and as additional components in broader social programs, but inadequate uptake more broadly in the planning and implementation of bilateral projects.

Canada has supported the participation of Canadian Aboriginal people on its delegations for international negotiations, such as those under the *Convention on Biological Diversity*. However, Aboriginal groups have expressed concerns about their lack of ability to directly participate in the setting of Canadian international negotiating positions on issues affecting them.

10.5 ENVIRONMENT

As indicated in Canada's Foreign Policy, *Canada and the World* (1995), six program priorities have been identified for Canadian ODA, one of which is the need to help developing countries to protect their environment and to contribute to addressing global and regional environmental issues. CIDA's 1992 *Policy on Environmental Sustainability* has resulted in a substantial number of environment projects focused on capacity-building in developing countries and countries with economies in transition. In 2000-2001, slightly less than 10 per cent of CIDA ODA disbursements related to the environment. Despite this substantial level of environmental programming, environmental analysis has not been systematically integrated into all aspects of program decision-making, with the exception of environmental review procedures.

Canada has been, and continues to be, a supporter of the Global Environment Facility (GEF), which is the only multi-convention financial mechanism (UNFCCC, CBD and POPs) emerging after the Earth Summit 1992. Canada ranks 7th among the donor countries that contribute to the GEF, and actively participates in the work of the GEF Council. Canada is also a significant contributor to the Multilateral Fund under the Montreal Protocol.

In 2000, Canada allocated $100 million for the Canada Climate Change Development Fund to address causes and effects of climate change in developing countries and countries with economies in transition. Out of this amount, Canada has allocated $10 million to the LDC Fund for National Climate Change Adaptation Programs under the UNFCCC. It has also invested an additional US$10 million in the World Bank Prototype Carbon Fund, and allocated $20 million to the World Bank to support capacity building in developing countries and countries with economies in transition to manage persistent organic pollutants.

10.6 DESERTIFICATION

Canada played an active role in the negotiation of the *Convention to Combat Desertification* after Rio, ratified it in 1995, and has continued to be actively involved in its implementation, primarily in west, east and southern Africa. Canada currently occupies the Presidency of the Conference of Parties to the UNCCD, a two-year mandate (to 2003). CIDA, in collaboration with IDRC and a number of NGOs, including Solidarité Canada-Sahel and USC Canada, have supported implementation of the *Convention* in developing countries. Solidarité Canada-Sahel currently coordinates the International NGO Network on Desertification (le Réseau international d'ONG sur la désertification – RIOD). While IDRC has focused its efforts on fostering local community participation in national desertification action plans, and on building local capacity, CIDA has addressed land degradation through natural resources management. In 2000-2001 the total value of bilateral projects contributing in whole or in part to combating desertification, was approximately $500 million. The figures do not include the portion of Canada's multilateral contributions to such bodies as the FAO, UNDP, UNEP, the CGIAR research centres, the GEF and IFAD, whose programs include an emphasis on combating desertification, nor to the Convention's Secretariat and Global Mechanism.

10.7 CONTINUING CHALLENGES

Canadian performance on international cooperation is a touchstone for its commitment to make an increasingly global world more sustainable. The important commitments remain partly unfulfilled for finance and technology transfer to developing countries made by Canada and other OECD countries at Rio, to incorporate developing countries better into the international trading system, and to address continuing high levels of poverty in many parts of the world. The most significant challenges for Canada are to make a difference in poverty reduction efforts in developing countries through focused development cooperation and increased and well-targeted direct investment; to pursue non-discriminatory approaches to integrate environment, labour and human rights elements into the evolving set of international trade agreements; and to ensure coherence in domestic and in international policies that touch on these efforts in order to maximize synergies among international trade, investment and development cooperation efforts.

As a peaceful, prosperous country with a large landbase, Canadians are better able than most to make the investments required to enhance the sustainability of their lifestyles. During the last decade, they have achieved much: they are wealthier, use energy and resources more efficiently, have improved their governments' finances, emit fewer toxic chemicals into the environment, protect more landscapes, manage forests more sustainably and have achieved one of the world's highest standard of living as calculated by the UN's Human Development Index. Internationally, Canada has played a leading role in peacekeeping and in developing important international agreements (such as Persistent Organic Pollutants and Straddling Fish Stocks). In addition, it has forgiven the debt of several very poor countries.

In spite of these achievements Canada continues to face challenges related to all aspects of sustainable development. Among the continuing challenges are the needs to reduce pollution, preserve ecological integrity of natural capital, and reduce urban encroachment onto surrounding lands. Disparities remain in equity among social groups, among regions and between genders, although gaps have been reduced. The situation of Aboriginal people is of particular concern.

On the positive side, efforts are ongoing to ensure that international trade agreements integrate the needs of developing countries and environmental, labour, and broad social considerations. However, Canada's contribution to foreign aid has diminished even as the standard of living of Canadians has improved.

While Canadian governments at all levels, Aboriginal people, labour, many corporations, communities and NGOs have implemented a large number of initiatives that should produce positive impacts in the years ahead, many of these actions will not make their mark for some time to come. For example, it will take time before reductions in emissions of some toxic substances translate into decreases in soil, water or country food concentrations; or for changes in silviculture to be noticed in ecosystem health; or for a healthier environment to have a noticeable effect on the health of Canadians.

The lag-time between action and result is particularly evident in the many changes in decision-making processes and management practices that governments and civil society have initiated. While these changes are essential, the impact of implementing strategic environmental assessment in a government, or an environmental management system in a company, for example, will not be felt fully for years. To a large extent, it is therefore premature to assess their impact at this stage.

Another reason why it is difficult to evaluate the impact of measures taken is that the information required to do so is often unavailable. During the 1990s, Canada made a major investment to improve the development and dissemination of health data. In the environmental area, a Canadian Information System for the Environment is at the beginning stages and it will take years before the needed investments in information gathering and analysis yield more up-to-date knowledge of Canada's state of the environment. The problem is different in the social area where detailed data exist but a conceptual framework to measure social sustainability is still missing.

Initiatives To Improve Environmental Information

- In 2000, the National Round Table on the Environment and the Economy (NRTEE), an advisory body to the Prime Minister, launched its Environment and Sustainable Development Indicators (ESDI) Initiative. ESDI is a three-year program to develop and promote a set of national indicators of natural, produced and human capital.
- The federal government stopped producing a national state of the environment report in 1996 but has continued to publish indicators on specific environmental issues and has begun to design a Canadian Information System for the Environment. In the past two years, Canada has published national status reports on sustainable forest management, wildlife species and protected areas. Yukon, Saskatchewan, Quebec and British Columbia each produce periodic state of the environment reports.
- NGOs have developed Genuine Progress Indicator sets for Alberta and Nova Scotia.
- Canadian policy research groups are developing Quality of Life Indicators.

Despite the limitations imposed by incomplete and inconsistent data and the lack of agreed upon performance metrics, it can be concluded that Canada's overall sustainable development performance is consistent with that of most of its industrialized peers: its standard of living, its ecological footprint, the longevity and educational attainment of its inhabitants are all broadly comparable to those of G7 countries.

While it is hard to answer in detail how well Canada is doing in its progress toward more sustainable forms of development, the much more difficult – and equally important – question is: Is Canada doing well enough? That question cannot be answered here, although it is hoped that this report provides some of the information and the range of perspectives required to begin to address this fundamental question.

SELECTED BIBLIOGRAPHY

Chapter 2: Changes to Decision-Making Structures and Processes

Canadian Institute for Environmental Law and Policy. 2001. *Sustainable Development in Canada: A New Federal Plan.* CIELAP: Toronto, Ontario.

Canadian Youth Summit Team. 2001. *Ministry of Holism: National and International Governance for Sustainability – A Position Paper.*

Conseil des ministres de l'Éducation (Canada). *Une Éducation Qui Favorise La Viabilité.*

Council of Ministers of Education, Canada. 1999. *Educating for Sustainability: The Status of Sustainable Development Education in Canada.* www.cmec.ca/else/environment.en.pdf.

Innovation and Partnership Federal Government Working Group. 2001. *Federal Government Initiatives Since 1992.*

IUCN Commission in Education and Communication. 2001. *Education for Sustainable Development.*

Chapter 3: Social Sustainability

Battle, Ken (Caledon Institute of Social Policy). 1999. *Poverty Eases Slightly.* www.caledoninst.org/

Canadian Council on Social Development. 1998. *Will the 1998 Federal Budget Bring Down Canada's Social Deficit?* www.ccsd.ca/pr/pp_bud98.htm

DFAIT. *Canada and the World Summit for Social Development.* www.dfait-maeci.gc.ca/english/foreignp/social/sommet.htm

Human Resources Development Canada. 1998. *Distribution of Family Incomes Across Regions in Canada.* www.hrdc-drhc.gc.ca/sp-ps/arb-dgra/publications/research/1999docs/w-98-3e.pdf

Lee, Kevin K. 2000. *Urban Poverty in Canada.* www.ccsd.ca/pubs/2000/up/

Manitoba Education, Training and Youth. 2000. *Education for a Sustainable Future: A Resource for Curriculum Developers, Teachers, and Administrators.*

Rees, William. 1996. *Revisiting Carrying Capacity: Area-Based Indicators of Sustainability.* http://dieoff.org/page110.htm

Torjman, Sherri (Caledon Institute of Social Policy). 2000. *The Social Dimension of Sustainable Development.* http://www.caledoninst.org/

UN. *Fourth World Conference on Women – Beijing Declaration.* www.un.org/womenwatch/daw/beijing/platform/declar.htm

Chapter 4: Sustainable Communities

AFN/INAC Joint Initiative for Policy Development (Lands and Trust Services). 2000. *Banishing the Indian Agent. Choices for Change: Restoring First Nation Governments.*

AFN/INAC Joint Initiative for Policy Development (Lands and Trust Services). 1999. *Environment Research Paper and Focus Group Reports.*

Canadian Urban Transit Association (2001) Trans-Action 2001 http://cutaactu.ca/TransAction2001.pdf

CMHC and Environment Canada. 1996. Measuring Urban Sustainability: Canadian Indicators Workshop.

Government of Canada. *Canadian Rural Partnership: Rural Canadians Speak Out – Summary of Rural Dialogue Input for the National Rural Workshop.* www.rural.gc.ca/discpaper_e.phtml

Green Communities Association. 2000. Green Communities in Profile.
http://www.gca.ca/PROFILES.pdf

Indian and Northern Affairs Canada. 2001. *Gathering Strength – Canada's Aboriginal Action Plan: A Progress Report.*

Sustainable Communities Federal Government Working Group. 2001. *Sustainable Communities Theme: Earth Summit 2002.*

Chapter 5: Health and Environment

Canadian Centre for Pollution Prevention and Environment Canada. 2000. *Report to the Ninth Meeting of the United Nations Commission on Sustainable Development on the International Pollution Prevention Summit.*

Hancock, Dr. Trevor. 2000. *Indicators of Environmental Health in the Urban Setting: A Report for the IJC Conference on Environmental Health Indicators.*
http://ottserver1.ottawa.ijc.org/hptf/concen/papers/UrbanIndic1.pdf

Health and Environment Federal Government Working Group. 2001. *2002 Earth Summit: A Retrospective Look at Canadian Approaches to Health and Environment Since Rio.*

Chapter 6: Conservation and Stewardship of Biodiversity

Conservation and Stewardship Federal Government Working Group. 2001. *A Decade of Sustainable Developments: Canada's Progress Since 1992.*

Environment Canada. 1998. *Caring for Canada's Biodiversity: Canada's First National Report to the Conference of the Parties to the Convention on Biological Diversity.*
http://www.cbin.ec.gc.ca/cbin/Html/en/Input/BCODocuments/2957_Caring_f_E.pdf

Environment Canada. *Species at Risk: Backgrounders.*
www.speciesatrisk.gc.ca/species/sar/media/back1_e.htm

Federal Provincial Parks Council. *Working Together: Parks and Protected Areas in Canada.*
http://parkscanada.pch.gc.ca/library/fppc/english/fppcreport_e.pdf

Government of Canada. 1998. *Caring for Canada's Biodiversity: Annex to Canada's First National Report to the Conference of the Parties to the Convention on Biological Diversity – Inventory of Initiatives.* Hull, Quebec.

Hackman, Arlin. 2000. *Canada's Endangered Spaces Campaign* (presented at Beyond the Trees: An International Conference on the Design and Management of Forest Protected Areas).
www.panda.org/forests4life/spotlights/trees/bt_arpaper.htm

Lindgren, Richard D. 2001. *The Species at Risk Act: An Overview.* http://www.cela.ca/408sara.pdf

Natural Resources Canada. 1997. *Safeguarding Our Assets, Securing Our Future.*
http://www.nrcan.gc.ca/dmo/susdev/html/english/tofc_e.html

Wildlife Habitat Canada. 2001. *The Status of Wildlife Habitats in Canada.*
http://www.whc.org/whc/WHCDocuments.nsf/Documents?OpenFrameSet

World Wildlife Fund. 2000. *Endangered Spaces: The Wilderness Campaign That Changed the Canadian Landscape.*

Chapter 7: Sustainable Development of Natural Resources

Fisheries and Oceans Canada. 1997. *Ensuring the Health of the Oceans and Other Seas (Monograph No. 3).* http://www.ec.gc.ca/agenda21/97/mono3.htm

Environment Canada. 1997. *National Environmental Indicator Series: Forest Biodiversity.*
www2.ec.gc.ca/ind/English/For_Bio/default.cfm

Environment Canada. 1998. *Canada and Freshwater: Experience and Practices (Monograph No 6).*
http://www.ec.gc.ca/soer-ree/english/Indicators/Issues/For_Bio/default.cfm

Environment Canada. *National Environmental Indicator Series: Sustaining Canada's Forests.*
www2.ec.gc.ca/soer-ree/English/Indicators/Issues/Forest/default.cfm

National Roundtable on the Environment and the Economy. 1997. National Civil Society Consultations on Energy Issues, Oceans Issues, and Forestry Issues for Rio+5.
www.ecouncil.ac.cr/rio/national/reports/america/canada.htm

Natural Resources Canada. 1995. *Sustainable Development and Minerals and Metals.*
www.nrcan.gc.ca/mms/sdev/sdemain.pdf

Natural Resources Canada. 1997. *Sustainable Development of Minerals and Metals (Monograph No. 4).* http://www.ec.gc.ca/agenda21/97/mono4.htm

Natural Resources Canada. 1997. *Sustainable Management of Forests (Monograph No. 1)*. http://www.ec.gc.ca/agenda21/97/mono1.htm

Natural Resources Canada. 2000. *Criteria and Indicators of Sustainable Forest Management in Canada*. http://www.nrcan.gc.ca/cfs/proj/ppiab/ci/2000pdf/full_report_e.pdf

Natural Resources Canada. 2000. *Minerals and Metals: Towards a Sustainable Future (Monograph No. 10)*. http://www.ec.gc.ca/agenda21/2000/minerals.htm

Natural Resources Canada. 2000. *Sustainable Forest Management: A Continued Commitment in Canada (Monograph No. 9)*. http://www.ec.gc.ca/agenda21/2000/foresteng.htm

Natural Resources Canada. 2000. *The Path Forward to Sustainable Development Strategy 2000*. www.nrcan.gc.ca/dmo/susdev/sd2k/sd2ktoce.htm

Natural Resources Canada. 2000. *The State of Canada's Forests 1999-2000 – Forests in the New Millennium*. http://nrcan.gc.ca/cfs/proj/ppiab/sof/sof00/toc.shtml

Natural Resources Canada. 2001. *The State of Canada's Forests 2000-2001 – Sustainable Forestry: A Reality in Canada*. http://www.nrcan-rncan.gc.ca/cfs-scf/national/what-quoi/sof/latest_e.html.

Chapter 8: Climate Change

David Suzuki Foundation. 2000. *Dangerous Atmosphere: Canada's negotiating position threatens the climate*. www.davidsuzuki.org/files/PositionPaper.pdf

Environment Canada. 1997. *Greenhouse Gas Emissions Outlook to 2020*. www2.ec.gc.ca/climate/fact/greenhou.html

Environment Canada. 2000. *Canada's Greenhouse Gas Inventory 1990-1998: Final Submission to the UNFCCC Secretariat*. www.ec.gc.ca/pdb/ghg/ghg_docs/CGHGI_00Vol1_Web_Eng.pdf Appendices: www.ec.gc.ca/pdb/ghg/ghg_docs/CGHGI_00Vol2_Web_Eng.pdf

Environment Canada. *National Environmental Indicator Series: Climate Change*. www2.ec.gc.ca/ind/English/Climate/default.cfm

IISD. 1998. *A Guide to Kyoto: Climate Change and What it Means to Canadians*. http://iisd.ca/pdf/kyotoprimer_en.pdf

Natural Resources Canada. 2001. *Government of Canada's Climate Change Initiatives*.

Office of Energy Efficient (NRCan). 2000. *The State of Energy Efficiency in Canada*. www.oee.nrcan.gc.ca/see/index.cfm

Bibliography

Chapter 9: The Canadian Arctic

Arctic Council. 2001. *Arctic Submission for Canada's National Assessment Report, World Summit on Sustainable Development.*

Arctic Monitoring and Assessment Program. 1997. *Arctic Pollution Issues: A State of the Arctic Environment Report.* http://www.amap.no/assess/soaer-cn.htm

Canadian Arctic Resources Committee. 2000. *Persistent Organic Pollutants: Are we close to a solution?* www.indelta.com/cgibin2/carcpub.cgi? http://www.carc.org/pubs/fall2000/Northern_Perspectives_26.pdf

Environment Canada. 2000. *Indigenous Peoples and Sustainable Development in the Canadian Arctic (Monograph No. 11).* http://www.ec.gc.ca/agenda21/2000/indigenous.htm

Chapter 10: International Cooperation

CIDA. 2001. *Performance Report.*

CIDA. 2001. *Strengthening Aid Effectiveness: New Approaches to Canada's International Assistance Program.*

CIDA. Statistical Report on Official Development Assistance Fiscal Year 1999-2000. http://www.acdi-cida.gc.ca/desertification-e.htm

CIDA. *1992-93 Estimates; 1995-96 Estimates; 2001-2002 Estimates.*

CIDA. *Canada's First Official Report on the Implementation of the Convention to Combat Desertification.* www.acdi-cida.gc.ca/cida_ind.nsf/ and click on English-Desertification in the list of publications.

Commissioner of the Environment and Sustainable Development. Database of Canada's International Environmental Commitments. http://pubx.dfait-maeci.gc.ca/A_Branch/AES/Env_commitments.nsf

Department of Foreign Affairs and International Trade. *Global Agenda.* www.dfait-maeci.gc.ca/english/NEWS/NEWSLETR/GLOBAL/table1.htm

IDRC. 2001. *Toward Sustainable and Equitable Development: A Decade of Progress at IDRC Since Rio.*

Commissioned Papers for the preparation of Canada's National Report

(all papers are available at: www.canada2002earthsummit.gc.ca or www.canada2002sommetdelaterre.gc.ca)

Bell, David V.J. and Michelle Grinstein. 2001. *Sustainable Urban Communities in Canada: From Rio to Johannesburg.*

Bramley, Matthew. 2001. *Contribution on Climate Change to the Canadian National Assessment for the*

World Summit on Sustainable Development.

Brooke, Lorraine. 2001. *Arctic Submission for Canada's National Assessment Report, World Summit on Sustainable Development.*

Bruce, James P. 2001. *Canada's Response to Climate Change – A Work in Progress.*

Cosbey, Aaron. 2001. *Trade, Markets and Economic Policy: Charting Canada's Progress on Sustainable Development Commitments Related to Trade and Investment.*

Forest Products Association of Canada. 2001. *Towards a Sustainable Canadian Forest Products Industry: Implementing Agenda 21.*

Green, David M. 2001. *Endangered Species in Canada.*

Griss, Paul. 2001. *Canada's National Assessment Report, World Summit on Sustainable Development: A Commentary on Sustainable Forest Management in Canada (1992-2002).*

Hancock, Dr. Trevor. 2001. *Health, Environment and Sustainable Development: The Child Health Perspective.*

International Council for Local Environmental Initiatives (ICLEI). 2001. *Sustainable Communities Report.*

Kassi, Norma. 2001. *Progress in Canada's North on Sustainable Development Since the Rio Earth Summit 1992: An Aboriginal Perspective on the Yukon.*

May, Elizabeth E, LLB, DHL. 2001. *The Role of Civil Society: Pre and Post Rio.*

Mining Association of Canada. 2001. *World Summit on Sustainable Development, Submission for the Canada National Assessment Report by the Mining Association of Canada (MAC).*

Telford, Laura. 2001. *Conserving Canada's Biodiversity – Putting the Pieces Together: Moving From Planning to Implementation.*

The Conference Board of Canada. 2001. *Submission to Canada's National Assessment Report, World Summit on Sustainable Development.*

The Delphi Group. 2001. *Canada's National Assessment Report: Health and the Environment.*

Tomlinson, Brian. 2001. *Agenda 21 and Canadian International Cooperation: A Progress Report for Rio +10.*

Wood, Bernard. 2001. *Canada's National Assessment Report, World Summit for Sustainable Development: International Cooperation.*

Young, Alan. 2001. *Mineral Development and Sustainability – Measuring our Progress Since Rio.*

Sustainable Development Strategies

The following federal government departments and agencies are required to prepare sustainable development strategies:

Agriculture and Agri-FoodCanada
http://www.agr.ca/policy/environment/eb/public_html/pdfs/sds/SDSII-english.pdf

Atlantic Canada Opportunities Agency
http://www.acoa-apeca.gc.ca/e/library/reports/sustainable2.pdf

Canada Customs and Revenue Agency (formerly Revenue Canada)
http://www.ccra-adrc.gc.ca/agency/sustainable/toc-e.html

Canadian Heritage, Department of
http://www.pch.gc.ca/sds/

Canadian International Development Agency
http://w3.acdi-cida.gc.ca/sds

Citizenship and Immigration Canada
http://www.cic.gc.ca/english/policy/sds/index/html

Economic Development Agency of Canada for the Regions of Quebec
http://www.dec-ced.gc.ca/en/pdf/sdd.pdf

Environment Canada
http://www.ec.gc.ca/sd-dd_consult/pdf/sds2001_2003_final_e.pdf

Finance Canada, Department of
http://www.fin.gc.ca/toce/2001/sds2001e.html

Fisheries and Oceans Canada
http://www.dfo-mpo.gc.ca/sds-sdd/strategy_e.htm

Foreign Affairs and International Trade, Department of
http://www.dfait-maeci.gc.ca/sustain/SustainDev/10855_DFAIT_S.D._Ev8.pdf

Health Canada
http://www.hc-sc.gc.ca/susdevdur/sds_2000e.pdf

Human Resources Development Canada
http://www.hrdc-drhc.gc.ca/dept/sds/toc.shtml

Indian and Northern Affairs Canada
http://www.ainc-inac.gc.ca/pr/sus/sds01_e.pdf

Industry Canada
http://strategis.ic.gc.ca/SSG/sd00228e.html

Justice Canada, Department of
http://canada.justice.gc.ca/en/dept/pub/sds/index.html

National Defence
http://www.dnd.ca/admie/dge/sds/SDS00_E.pdf

Natural Resources Canada
http://www.nrcan-rncan.gc.ca/dmo/susdev/pdf/future.pdf

Parks Canada Agency (prepared and tabled its first strategy in February 2001)
http://www.parkscanada.gc.ca/Library/DownloadDocuments/DocumentsArchive/sustdevstra_e.pdf

Public Works and Government Services Canada
http://www.pwgsc.gc.ca/sd-env/text/home-e.html

Solicitor General Canada
http://www.sgc.gc.ca/epub/othpub/esustainable/esustainable2000.htm

Transport Canada
http://www.tc.gc.ca/envaffairs/english/SDStrategy/2001.htm

Treasury Board of Canada Secretariat
http://www.tbs-sct.gc.ca/pubs_pol/partners/sds-sdd1_e.html

Veterans Affairs Canada
http://www.vac-acc.gc.ca/content/department/reports/susdev2001e.pdf

Western Economic Diversification Canada
http://www.wd.gc.ca/eng/rpts/strategies/sd_plan/sd2000/default.htm

The following four organizations have voluntarily prepared strategies and tabled them in the House of Commons:

Canadian Environmental Assessment Agency
http://www.ceaa.gc.ca/0012/0004/development2001_e.htm

Correctional Service Canada
http://www.csc-scc.gc.ca/text/pblct/sustain/sds_e.pdf

Office of the Auditor General of Canada
http://www.oag-bvg.gc.ca/domino/reports.nsf/html/0035ce.html

Royal Canadian Mounted Police
http://www.rcmp-grc.gc.ca/html/sustain1.htm

Miscellaneous

Auditor General of Canada. 1991-2001. *Report of the Auditor General of Canada to the House of Commons.* Ottawa, Ontario. http://www.oag-bvg.gc.ca/domino/other.nsf/html/99repm_e.html

Boyd, David R. 2001. *Canada vs. The OECD: An Environmental Comparison.* http://www.environmentalindicators.com/htdocs/execsum.htm

Commissioner of the Environment and Sustainable Development. 1997-2001. *Report of the Commissioner of the Environment and Sustainable Development.* Ottawa, Ontario. http://www.oag-bvg.gc.ca/domino/cesd_cedd.nsf/html/menu3_e.html

Commission for Environmental Cooperation. 2001. *The North American Mosaic: A State of the Environment Report.* http://www.cec.org/files/PDF/PUBLICATIONS/soe_en.pdf

Department of Finance. 2001. *Economic Update.* http://www.fin.gc.ca/ec2001/ec01e.pdf

Department of Finance. 2000. *Economic Statement and Budget Update.* http://www.fin.gc.ca/ec2000/pdf/overe.pdf

DFAIT. (1996 or 1997). *The Commission on Sustainable Development: Canadian Country Profile.* http://www.dfait-maeci.gc.ca/english/foreignp/environ/AGE3-01E.HTM

Environmental Commissioner of Ontario Annual Reports. 1997, 1998, 1999/2000. http://www.eco.on.ca/english/publicat/index.htm

Environment Canada. 2001. *Tracking Key Environmental Issues.* Ottawa, Ontario. www.ec.gc.ca/TKEI/eng_final.pdf

Government of Canada. 1994-1996. *Report of Canada to the United Nations Commission on Sustainable Development.* Ottawa, Ontario.
1994:www.ec.gc.ca/agenda21/uneng1.html
1995:www.ec.gc.ca/agenda21/uneng.html
1996:www.ec.gc.ca/agenda21/96/hompgeng.html

Government of Canada. 1997. *Building Momentum: Sustainable Development in Canada – Canada's Submission to the Fifth Session of the UNCSD.* Ottawa, Ontario. www.ec.gc.ca/agenda21/97/content.htm.

Government of Canada. 1991, 1996. *The State of Canada's Environment.* Ottawa, Ontario. 1996: www.ec.gc.ca/soer-ree/English/1996Report/Doc/1-1.cfm

OECD. 2000. Policy Brief: Economic Survey of Canada, 2000. www1.oecd.org/publications/Pol_brief/economic_surveys/e-canada.pdf

OECD. 2001. Policy Brief: Economic Survey of Canada, 2001. http://webnet1.oecd.org/pdf/M00009000/M00009732.pdf

Projet de Société. 1994. *Canada and Agenda 21.* http://www.iisd.org/worldsd/canada/projet/a21toc.htm

Rees, William. 1999. *Population and our ecological footprint.* CBC – The Magazine Viewpoint. www.cbc.ca/news/national/viewpoint/view991012.html

Sierra Club of Canada. 2001. *Rio Report Card.* www.sierraclub.ca/national/rio/

Statistics Canada. 2000. *Econnections: Linking the Environment and the Economy.*

Sustainable Development: A Canadian Perspective